TINY ALICE
was originally published by
Atheneum Publishers.

Plays by Edward Albee

*All Over
 The American Dream
*Box and Quotations from Chairman Mao Tse-tung
 The Death of Bessie Smith
*A Delicate Balance
 The Sandbox
*Tiny Alice
*Who's Afraid of Virginia Woolf?
 The Zoo Story

Adaptations

The Ballad of the Sad Cafe
      (from the novella by Carson McCullers)
*Everything in the Garden
      (from the play by Giles Cooper)
 Malcolm
      (from the novel by James Purdy)

*Published by POCKET BOOKS

TINY ALICE

Edward Albee

PUBLISHED BY POCKET BOOKS NEW YORK

TINY ALICE

Atheneum edition published 1965

POCKET BOOK edition published April, 1966

7th printing.....................January, 1974

This POCKET BOOK edition includes every word contained in the original, higher-priced edition. It is printed from brand-new plates made from completely reset, clear, easy-to-read type. POCKET BOOK editions are published by POCKET BOOKS, a division of Simon & Schuster, Inc., 630 Fifth Avenue, New York, N.Y. 10020. Trademarks registered in the United States and other countries.

FOR

NOEL FARRAND

AUTHOR'S NOTE

It has been the expressed hope of many that I would write a preface to the published text of *Tiny Alice*, clarifying obscure points in the play—explaining my intention, in other words. I have decided against creating such a guide because I find—after reading the play over—that I share the view of even more people: that the play is quite clear. I will confess, though, that *Tiny Alice* is less opaque in reading than it would be in any single viewing. One further note: this printed text of *Tiny Alice* represents the complete play. Some deletions—mainly in the final act—were made for the New York production; and while I made the deletions myself, and quite cheerfully, realizing their wisdom in the particular situation, I restore them here with even greater enthusiasm.

EDWARD ALBEE

FIRST PERFORMANCE

December 29, 1964, New York City, Billy Rose Theatre

LAWYER	*William Hutt*
CARDINAL	*Eric Berry*
JULIAN	*John Gielgud*
BUTLER	*John Heffernan*
MISS ALICE	*Irene Worth*

DIRECTED BY *Alan Schneider*

SETS BY *William Ritman*

GOWNS BY *Mainbocher*

LIGHTING BY *Martin Aronstein*

ACT ONE

Scene One

(The CARDINAL'S *garden. What is needed . . . ? Ivy climbing a partial wall of huge stones? An iron gate? Certainly two chairs—one, the larger, obviously for His Eminence; the other, smaller—and certainly an elaborate birdcage, to stage left, with some foliage in it, and two birds, cardinals . . . which need not be real. At rise, the* LAWYER *is at the birdcage, talking to the birds)*

LAWYER

Oomm, yoom, yoom, um? Tick-tick-tick-tick-tick. Um? You do-do-do-do-do-um? Tick-tick-tick-tick-tick-tick-tick-um? *(He raises his fingers to the bars)* Do-do-do-do-do-do-do? Aaaaaawwwww! Oomm, yoom, yoom, um?
(The CARDINAL *enters from stage right—through the iron gates?—unseen by the* LAWYER, *who repeats some of the above as the* CARDINAL *moves toward center)*

CARDINAL
(Finally. Quietly amused)
Saint Francis?

LAWYER
(Swinging around; flustered; perhaps more annoyed than embarrassed at being discovered)
Your Eminence!

CARDINAL
Our dear Saint Francis, who wandered in the fields and forests, talked to all the . . .

1

LAWYER
(Moving to kiss the ring)
Your Eminence, we appreciate your kindness in taking
the time to see us; we know how heavy a schedule
you . . .

CARDINAL
*(Silencing him by waving his ring at him. The
LAWYER kneels, kisses the ring, rises)*
We are pleased . . . we are pleased to be your servant
(Trailing off) . . . if . . . we can be your servant. We
addressed you as Saint Francis . . .

LAWYER *(Properly mumbling)*
Oh, but surely . . .

CARDINAL
. . . as Saint Francis . . . who did talk to the birds so,
did he not. And here we find *you*, who talk not only to
the birds but to *(With a wave at the cage)*—you must forgive us—to cardinals as well. *(Waits for reaction, gets
none, tries again)* . . . To cardinals? As well?

LAWYER *(A tight smile)*
We . . . we understood.

CARDINAL *(He, too)*
Did we.
(A brief silence, as both smiles hold)

LAWYER
(To break it, moving back toward the cage)
We find it droll—if altogether appropriate in this setting
—that there should be two cardinals . . . uh, together
. . . *(Almost a sneer)* . . . in conversation, as it were.

CARDINAL *(The smile again)*

Ah, well, they are a comfort to each other . . . companionship. And they have so much to say. They . . . understand each other so much better than they would . . . uh, *other* birds.

LAWYER

Indeed. And so much better than they would understand saints?

CARDINAL
(Daring him to repeat it, but still amused)

Sir?

LAWYER *(Right in)*

That cardinals understand each *other* better than they understand saints.

CARDINAL *(Not rising to it)*

Who is to say? Will you sit?

LAWYER *(Peering into the cage)*

They are extraordinary birds . . . cardinals, if I may say so. . . .

CARDINAL *(Through with it)*

You push it too far, sir. Will you join us?
(He moves to his chair, sits in it)

LAWYER

(Brief pause, then surrender; moves to the other chair)

Of course.

CARDINAL *(A deep sigh)*

Well. What should we do now? *(Pause)* Should we clap our hands *(Does so, twice)* . . . twice, and have a monk

appear? A very old monk? With just a ring of white hair
around the base of his head, stooped, fast-shuffling, his
hands deep in his sleeves? Eh? And should we send him
for wine? Um? Should we offer you wine, and should we
send him scurrying off after it? Yes? Is that the scene you
expect now?

LAWYER
(Very relaxed, but pointed)
It's so difficult to know what to expect in a Cardinal's
garden, Your Eminence. An old monk would do . . . or
—who is to say?—perhaps some good-looking young
novice, all freshly scrubbed, with big working-class hands,
who would . . .

CARDINAL *(Magnanimous)*
We have both in our service; if a boy is more to your
pleasure . . .

LAWYER
I don't drink in the afternoon, so there is need for neither
. . . unless Your Eminence . . . ?

CARDINAL
*(His eyes sparkling with the joke to come about
his nature)*
We are known to be . . . ascetic, so we will have none
of it. Just . . . three cardinals . . . and Saint Francis.

LAWYER
Oh, not Saint Francis, not a saint. Closer to a king; closer
to Croesus. That was gibberish I was speaking to the
cardinals—and it's certainly not accepted that Saint
Francis spoke gibberish to his . . . parishioners . . .
intentional gibberish or otherwise.

CARDINAL
It is not accepted; no.

LAWYER

No. May I smoke?

CARDINAL

Do.

LAWYER *(Lights up)*

Closer to Croesus; to gold; closer to wealth.

CARDINAL *(A heavy, weary sigh)*

Aahhhh, you *do* want to talk business, don't you?

LAWYER *(Surprisingly tough)*

Oh, come on, Your Eminence: *(Softer)* Do you want to spend the afternoon with me, making small talk? Shall we . . . shall we talk about . . . times gone by?

CARDINAL
(Thinks about it with some distaste)

No. No no; we don't think so. It wouldn't do. It's not charitable of us to say so, but when we were at school we did loathe you so.
(Both laugh slightly)

LAWYER

Your Eminence was not . . . beloved of everyone himself.

CARDINAL
(Thinking back, a bit smugly)

Ah, no; a bit out of place; out of step.

LAWYER

A swine, I thought.

CARDINAL

And we you.
(Both laugh a little again)

LAWYER

Do you ever slip?

CARDINAL

Sir?

LAWYER

Mightn't you—if you're not careful—*(Tiny pause)* lapse
. . . and say *I* to me . . . not we?

CARDINAL
(Pretending sudden understanding)
Ah *ha!* Yes, we under*stand.*

LAWYER

Do we, do we.

CARDINAL

We do. We—and here we speak of our*selves* and not of
our station—we . . . *we* reserve the first-person singular
for intimates . . . and equals.

LAWYER

. . . And your superiors.

CARDINAL
(Brushing away a gnat)
The case does not apply.

LAWYER
(Matter-of-factly; the vengeance is underneath)
You'll grovel, Buddy. *(Slaps his hip hard)* As automati-
cally and naturally as people slobber on that ring of
yours. As naturally as that, I'll have you do your obei-
sance. *(Sweetly)* As you used to, old friend.

CARDINAL

We . . . *(Thinks better of what he was about to say)*

You *were* a swine at school. *(More matter-of-factly)* A cheat in your examinations, a liar in all things of any matter, vile in your personal habits—unwashed and indecent, a bully to those you could intimidate and a sycophant to everyone else. We remember you more clearly each moment. It is law you practice, is it not? We find it fitting.

LAWYER
(A mock bow, head only)
We are of the same school, Your Eminence.

CARDINAL
And in the same class . . . but not *of*. You have come far—in a worldly sense . . . from so little, we mean. *(Musing)* The law.

LAWYER
I speak plainly.

CARDINAL
You are plain. As from your beginnings.

LAWYER *(Quietly)*
Overstuffed, arrogant, pompous son of a profiteer. And a whore. You are in the Church, are you not? We find it fitting.

CARDINAL
(A burst of appreciative laughter)
You're *good!* You *are!* Still! Gutter, but good. But, in law . . . *(Leaves it unfinished with a gesture)* Ah! It comes back to us; it begins to. What did we call you at school? What name, what nickname did we have for you . . . all of us? What term of simple honesty and . . . rough affection did we have for you? *(Tapping his head impatiently)* It comes back to us.

LAWYER *(Almost a snarl)*
We had a name for you, too.

CARDINAL *(Dismissing it)*
Yes, yes, but we forget it.

LAWYER
Your Eminence was not always so . . . eminent.

CARDINAL *(Remembering)*
Hy-e . . . *(Relishing each syllable)* Hy-e-na. Hy. E. Na.
We recall.

LAWYER
(Close to break-through anger)
We are close to Croesus, Your Eminence. I've brought
gold with me . . . *(Leans forward)* money, Your Eminence.

CARDINAL *(Brushing it off)*
Yes, yes; later. Hy-e-na.

LAWYER *(A threat, but quiet)*
A great deal of money, Your Eminence.

CARDINAL
We hear you, and we will discuss your business shortly.
And why did we call you hyena . . . ?

LAWYER *(Quiet threat again)*
If Croesus goes, he takes the gold away.

CARDINAL *(Outgoing)*
But, Hyena, you are not Croesus; you are Croesus' emis-
sary. You will wait; the gold will wait.

LAWYER
Are you certain?

CARDINAL *(Ignoring the last)*

Ah, yes, it was in natural-science class, was it not? *(The* LAWYER *rises, moves away a little)* Was it not?

LAWYER

Considering your mother's vagaries, you were never certain of your true father . . . were you?

CARDINAL

Correct, my child: considering one's mother's vagaries, one was never certain of one's true father . . . was one? But then, my child, we embraced the Church; and we *know* our true father. *(Pause; the* LAWYER *is silent)* It was in natural-science class, eleven-five until noon, and did we not discover about the hyena . . .

LAWYER

More money than you've ever seen!

CARDINAL *(Parody; cool)*

Yum-yum. *(Back to former tone)* Did we not discover about the hyena that it was a most resourceful scavenger? That, failing all other food, it would dine on offal . . .

LAWYER *(Angrier)*

Millions!

CARDINAL *(Pressing on)*

. . . and that it devoured the wounded and the dead? We found that last the most shocking: the dead. But we were young. And what horrified us most—and, indeed, what gave us all the thought that the name was most fitting for yourself—

LAWYER *(Ibid.)*

Money!

CARDINAL

. . . was that to devour its dead, scavenged prey, it
would often chew into it . . .

LAWYER

MONEY, YOU SWINE!

CARDINAL
(Each word rising in pitch and volume)
. . . chew into it THROUGH THE ANUS????
(Both silent, breathing a little hard)

LAWYER *(Finally; softly)*

Bastard.

CARDINAL *(Quietly, too)*
And now that we have brought the past to mind, and
remembered what we could not exactly, shall we . . .
talk business?

LAWYER *(Softly; sadly)*
Robes the color of your mother's vice.

CARDINAL *(Kindly)*
Come. Let us talk business. You are a businessman.

LAWYER *(Sadly again)*

As are you.

CARDINAL
(As if reminding a child of something)
We are a Prince of the Church. Do you forget?

LAWYER
(Suddenly pointing to the cage; too offhand)
Are those two lovers? Do they mate?

CARDINAL
(Patronizing; through with games)
Come; let us talk business.

LAWYER *(Persisting)*
Is it true? Do they? Even cardinals?

CARDINAL *(A command)*
If you have money to give us . . . sit down and give it.

LAWYER
To the lay mind—to the cognoscenti it may be fact, accepted and put out of the head—but to the lay mind it's speculation . . . voyeuristic, perhaps, and certainly anti-Rome . . . mere speculation, but whispered about, even by the school children—indeed, as you must recall, the more . . . urbane of us wondered about the Fathers at school . . .

CARDINAL
. . . the more wicked . . .

LAWYER
. . . about their vaunted celibacy . . . among one another. Of course, we were at an age when everyone diddled everyone else . . .

CARDINAL
Some.

LAWYER
Yes, and I suppose it was natural enough for us to assume that the priests did too.

CARDINAL
(As if changing the subject)
You have . . . fallen away from the Church.

LAWYER
And into the arms of reason.

CARDINAL
(Almost thinking of something else)
An unsanctified union: not a marriage: a whore's bed.

LAWYER
A common-law marriage, for I am at law and, as you
say, common. But it is quite respectable these days.

CARDINAL
*(Tough; bored with the church play-acting;
heavy and tired)*
All right; that's enough. What's your business?

LAWYER
(Pacing a little, after an appreciative smile)
My employer . . . wants to give some of her money to
the Church.

CARDINAL
(Enthusiastic, but guarded)
Does she!

LAWYER
Gradually.

CARDINAL *(Understanding)*
Ah-ha.

LAWYER *(Offhand)*
A hundred million now.

CARDINAL *(No shown surprise)*
And the rest gradually.

LAWYER

And the same amount each year for the next twenty—a hundred million a year. She is not ill; she has no intention of dying; she is quite young, youngish; there is no . . . rush.

CARDINAL

Indeed not.

LAWYER

It is that she is . . . overburdened with wealth.

CARDINAL

And it weighs on her soul.

LAWYER

Her soul is in excellent repair. If it were not, I doubt she'd be making the gesture. It is, as I said, that she is overburdened with wealth, and it . . . uh . . .

CARDINAL
(Finding the words for him)

. . . piles up.

LAWYER *(A small smile)*

. . . and it is . . . wasted . . . lying about. It is one of several bequests—arrangements—she is making at the moment.

CARDINAL
(Not astonishment, but unconcealed curiosity)

One of several?

LAWYER

Yes. The Protestants as well, the Jews . . . hospitals, universities, orchestras, revolutions here and there . . .

CARDINAL

Well, we think it is a . . . responsible action. She is
well, as you say.

LAWYER

Oh, yes; very.

CARDINAL

We are . . . glad. *(Amused fascination)* How did you
become her . . . lawyer, if we're not intruding upon . . . ?

LAWYER
(Brief pause; tight smile)
She had a dossier on me, I suppose.

CARDINAL

It must be a great deal less revealing than ours . . . than
our dossier on you.

LAWYER

Or a great deal *more* revealing.

CARDINAL

For her sake, and yours, we hope so.

LAWYER

To answer your question: I am a very good lawyer. It is
as simple as that.

CARDINAL *(Speculating on it)*
You *have* escaped prison.

LAWYER

I've done nothing to be imprisoned for.

CARDINAL

Pure. You're pure. You're ringed by stench, but you're

pure. Theres an odor that precedes you, and follows after
you're gone, but you walk in the eye of it . . . pure.

LAWYER *(Contemptuous)*

Look, pig, I don't enjoy you.

CARDINAL
(Mockingly; his arms wide as if for an embrace)
School chum!

LAWYER

If it were not my job to . . .

CARDINAL *(Abruptly)*

Well, it is! Do it!

LAWYER
(A smile to a hated but respected adversary)
I've given you the facts: a hundred million a year for
twenty years.

CARDINAL

But . . . ?

LAWYER *(Shrugs)*

That's all.

CARDINAL
(Stuttering with quiet excitement)
Y-y-y-y-yes, b-b-but shall I just go to the *house* and pick
it up in a *truck?*

LAWYER *(Great heavy relief)*

AAAAAAAHHHHHHHHhhhhhhhhh.

CARDINAL *(Caught up short)*

Hm? *(No reply)* HM???

LAWYER

Say it again. Say it once again for me.

CARDINAL *(Puzzled, suspicious)*

What? Say what?

LAWYER *(Leaning over him)*

Say it again; repeat what you said. It was a sweet sound.

CARDINAL *(Shouting)*

SAY WHAT!

LAWYER *(Cooing into his ear)*

"Yes, but shall I just go to the house and pick it up in a truck?"

CARDINAL
(Thinks on it a moment)

Well, perhaps there was a bit . . . perhaps there was too much levity there . . . uh, if one did not know one . . .

LAWYER *(Coos again)*

. . . "But shall *I* just go to the house . . ."

CARDINAL

Wh . . . NO!

LAWYER *(Sings it out)*

Shall IIIIIII just go!

CARDINAL *(Cross)*

No! We . . . we did not say that!

LAWYER

IIIIIIIIIIIII.

CARDINAL *(A threat)*

We did not say "I."

LAWYER *(Almost baby talk)*

We said I. Yes, we did; we said I. *(Suddenly loud and tough)* We said I, and we said it straight. I! I! I! By God, we picked up our skirts and lunged for it! IIIIIII! Me! Me! Gimme!

CARDINAL *(Full shout)*

WE SAID NO SUCH THING!

LAWYER *(Oily imitation)*

We reserve the first-person singular, do we not, for . . . for intimates, equals . . . or superiors. *(Harsher)* Well, my dear, you found all three applying. Intimate. How close would we rub to someone for all that wealth? As close as we once did?

CARDINAL
(Not wanting to hear, but weak)

Leave . . . leave off.

LAWYER *(Pressing)*

Equals? Oh, money equals anything you want. Levels! LEVELS THE EARTH! AND THE HEAVENS!

CARDINAL

ENOUGH!!

LAWYER *(The final thrust)*

. . . Or superiors. Who is superior, the one who stands on the mount of heaven? We think not! We have come down off our plural . . . when the stakes are high enough . . . and the hand, the kissed hand palsies out . . . FOR THE LOOT!!

CARDINAL *(Hissed)*

Satan!

LAWYER *(After a pause)*

Satan? You would believe it . . . if you believed in God. *(Breaks into—for lack of a better word—Satanic laughter, subsides. Patronizing now)* No, poor Eminence, you don't have to drive a truck around to the back door for it. We'll get the money to you . . . to your . . . people. Fact, I don't want you coming 'round . . . at all. Clacketing through the great corridors of the place, sizing it up, not content with enough wealth to buy off the first two hundred saints picked out of a bag, but wondering if *it* mightn't get thrown into the bargain as a . . . summer residence, perhaps . . . uh, after she dies and scoots up to heaven.

CARDINAL
(On his feet, but shaky, uncertain)

This . . . uh . . .

LAWYER

. . . interview is terminated?

CARDINAL *(Quietly)*

This is unseemly talk.

LAWYER *(Vastly, wryly amused)*

Oh? Is it?

CARDINAL
(A mechanical toy breaking down)

We will . . . we will forgive your presumption, your . . . excess . . . ex*cuse,* yes . . . excuse? . . . We will . . . overlook your . . . *(A plea is underneath)* Let us have no more of this talk. It *is* unseemly.

LAWYER
(Businesslike; as if the preceding speech had not happened)

As I said, I don't want you coming 'round . . . bothering her.

CARDINAL *(Humble)*

I would not bother the lady; I have not met her. Of course, I would very much like to have the pleasure of . . .

LAWYER

We slip often now, don't we.

CARDINAL *(Very soul-weary)*

Pardon?

LAWYER

The plural is gone out of us, I see.

CARDINAL

Ah. Well. Perhaps.

LAWYER

Regird yourself. We *are* about terminated. *(Quick, insulting finger-snaps)* Come! Come! Back up; back on your majesty! Hup!

CARDINAL

(Slowly, wearily coming back into shape)

Uh . . . yes . . . of—of course. We, uh, we shall make any arrangements you wish . . . naturally. We . . . we have no desire to intrude ourselves upon . . . uh . . . upon . . .

LAWYER

Miss Alice.

CARDINAL

Yes; upon Miss Alice. If she . . . if Miss Alice desires privacy, certainly her generosity has earned it for her. We . . . would not intrude.

LAWYER

You *are* kind. *(Fishing in a pocket for a notebook)* What
. . . is . . . your . . . secretary's . . . name . . . I
think I have it . . . right . . . *(Finds notebook)*

CARDINAL

Brother . . .

LAWYER

Julian! Is that not right?

CARDINAL

Yes, Brother Julian. He is an old friend of ours; we . . .

LAWYER

Rather daring of you, wasn't it? Choosing a lay brother
as your private secretary?

CARDINAL
(A combination of apology and defiance)
He is an old friend of ours, and he has served the . . .

LAWYER *(Praising a puppy)*
You are adventurous, are you not?

CARDINAL

He has been assigned many years to the . . .

LAWYER
(Waving his notebook a little)
We have it; all down; we know.

CARDINAL *(A little sadly)*

Ah-ha.

LAWYER

Yes. Well, we will send for your . . . Brother Julian.
. . . To clear up odds and ends. Every bank has its

runners. We don't ask vice presidents to . . . fetch and carry. Inform Your Brother Julian. We will send for him.
(LAWYER *exits*)

           CARDINAL *(To the exiting figure)*
Yes, we . . . will.
(Stands still, looks at the ground, tired, looks at his sleeves, his fingernails, his ring, up, out, over. Sighs, looks at the cage. Smiles slightly, moves to the cage, the fingers of his left hand fluttering at it)
Do . . . do you . . . do you have much to say to one another, my dears? Do you? You find it comforting? Hmmmmmmm? Do you? Hmmmm? Do-do-do-do-do-do-do-do? Hmmmmmm? Do?

CURTAIN

Scene Two

(The library of a mansion—a castle. Pillared walls, floor-to-ceiling leather-bound books. A great arched doorway, rear center. A huge reading table to stage left—practical. A phrenological head on it. To stage right, jutting out of the wings, a huge doll's-house model of the building of which the present room is a part. It is as tall as a man, and a good deal of it must be visible from all parts of the audience. An alternative—and perhaps more practical —would be for the arched doorway to be either left or right, with bookshelves to both sides of the set, coming toward the center, and to have the entire doll's house in the rear wall, in which case it could be smaller—say, twelve feet long and proportionately high. At any rate, it is essential. At rise, JULIAN is alone on stage, looking at the house)

JULIAN
(After a few moments of head-shaking concentration)
Extraordinary . . . extraordinary.

BUTLER
(After entering, observing JULIAN, not having heard him)
Extraordinary, isn't it?

JULIAN *(Mildly startled)*
Uh . . . yes, unbelievable . . . *(Agreeing)* Extraordinary.

BUTLER
(Who moves about with a kind of unbutlerlike ease)

I never cease to wonder at the . . . the fact of it, I
suppose.

JULIAN

The workmanship . . .

BUTLER *(A mild correction)*

That someone would do it.

JULIAN *(Seeing)*

Yes, yes.

BUTLER

That someone would . . . well, for heaven's sake, that
someone would build . . . *(Refers to the set)* . . . *this*
. . . castle? . . . and then . . . duplicate it in such
precise miniature, so exactly. Have you looked through
the windows?

JULIAN

No, I . . .

BUTLER

It is exact. Look and see.

JULIAN
*(Moves even closer to the model, peers through
a tiny window)*

Why . . . why, YES. I . . . there's a great . . . ba-
ronial dining room, even with tiny candlesticks on the
tables!

BUTLER
*(Nodding his head, a thumb back over his
shoulder)*

It's down the hall, off the hallway to the right.

JULIAN
(The proper words won't come)
It's . . . it's . . .

BUTLER
Look over here. There; right there.

JULIAN *(Peers)*
It's . . . it's this *room!* This room we're *in!*

BUTLER
Yes.

JULIAN
Extraordinary.

BUTLER
Is there anyone there? Are we there?

JULIAN
*Briefly startled, then laughs, looks back into
the model)*
Uh . . . no. It seems to be quite . . . empty.

BUTLER *(A quiet smile)*
One feels one should see one's self . . . almost.

JULIAN
*(Looks back to him; after a brief, thoughtful
pause)*
Yes. That would be rather a shock, wouldn't it?

BUTLER
Did you notice . . . did you notice that there is a model
within that room in the castle? A model of the model?

JULIAN
I . . . I did. But . . . I didn't register it, it seemed so
. . . continual.

BUTLER *(A shy smile)*

You don't suppose that within that tiny model in the
model there, there is . . . another room like this, with
yet a tinier model within it, and within . . .

JULIAN *(Laughs)*

. . . and within and within and within and . . . ? No, I
. . . rather doubt it. It's remarkable craftsmanship,
though. Remarkable.

BUTLER

Hell to clean.

JULIAN
(Conversational enthusiasm)

Yes! I should think so! Does it open from . . .

BUTLER

It's sealed. Tight. There is no dust.

JULIAN
(Disappointed at being joked with)

Oh.

BUTLER

I was sporting.

JULIAN

Oh.

BUTLER *(Straight curiosity)*

Did you mind?

JULIAN *(Too free)*

I? No!

BUTLER *(Doctrine, no sarcasm)*

It would almost be taken for granted—one would think—

that if a person or a person's surrogate went to the
trouble, *and* expense, of having such a dream toy made,
that the person *would* have it sealed, so that there'd be
no dust. Wouldn't one think.

JULIAN
(Sarcasm and embarrassment together)
One would think.

BUTLER
(After a pause, some rue)
I have enough to do as it is.

JULIAN
(Eager to move on to something else)
Yes, yes!

BUTLER
It's enormous . . . *(A sudden thought)* even for a castle,
I suppose. *(Points to the model)* Not that. *(Now to the
room)* This.

JULIAN
Endless! You . . . certainly you don't work alone.

BUTLER
Oh, Christ, no.

JULIAN *(Reaffirming)*
I would have *thought*.

BUTLER
(Almost daring him to disagree)
Still, there's enough work.

JULIAN *(Slightly testy)*
I'm *sure*.
(A pause between them)

BUTLER
(For no reason, a sort of "Oh, what the hell")
Heigh-ho.

JULIAN
Will there be . . . someone? . . . to see me? . . . soon?

BUTLER
Hm?

JULIAN
Will there be someone to see me soon! *(After a blank stare from the other)* You announced me? I trust?

BUTLER *(Snapping to)*
Oh! Yes! *(Laughs)* Sorry. Uh . . . yes, there will be someone to see you soon.

JULIAN
(Attempt at good-fellowship)
Ah, good!

BUTLER
Are you a priest?

JULIAN *(Self-demeaning)*
I? No, no . . .

BUTLER
If not Catholic, Episcopal.

JULIAN
No . . .

BUTLER
What, then?

JULIAN

I am a lay brother. I am not ordained.

BUTLER

You are *of* the cloth but have not taken it.

JULIAN *(None too happy)*

You *could* say that.

BUTLER *(No trifling)*

One *could* say it, and quite accurately. May I get you
some ice water?

JULIAN *(Put off and confused)*

No!

BUTLER *(Feigns apology)*

Sorry.

JULIAN

You must forgive me. *(Almost childlike enthusiasm)* This
is rather a big day for me.

BUTLER *(Nods understandingly)*

Iced *tea*.

JULIAN *(Laughs)*

No . . . nothing, thank you . . . uh . . . I don't have
your name.

BUTLER

Fortunate.

JULIAN

No, I meant that. . .

BUTLER

Butler.

JULIAN

Pardon?

BUTLER

Butler.

JULIAN

Yes. You . . . you *are* the butler, are you not, but . . .

BUTLER

Butler. My name is Butler.

JULIAN *(Innocent pleasure)*

How extraordinary!

BUTLER *(Putting it aside)*

No, not really. Appropriate: Butler . . . butler. If my
name were Carpenter, and I were a butler . . . or if I
were a carpenter, and my name were Butler . . .

JULIAN

But *still* . . .

BUTLER

. . . it would not be so appropriate. And think: if I were
a woman, and had become a chambermaid, say, and my
name were Butler . . .

JULIAN *(Anticipating)*

. . . you would be in for some rather tiresome exchanges.

BUTLER *(Cutting, but light)*

None more than this.

JULIAN *(Sadly)*

Aha.

BUTLER *(Forgiving)*

Coffee, then.

JULIAN *(As if he can't explain)*

No. Nothing.

BUTLER *(Semi-serious bow)*

I am at your service.

(LAWYER *enters)*

LAWYER

I, too.

JULIAN

Ah!

LAWYER

I'm sorry to have kept you waiting, but . . .

JULIAN

Oh, no, no . . .

LAWYER

. . . I was conferring with Miss Alice.

JULIAN

Yes.

LAWYER
(To BUTLER*; no fondness)*

Dearest.

BUTLER *(To* LAWYER*; same)*

Darling.

LAWYER *(To* JULIAN*)*

Doubtless, though, you two have . . . *(Waves a hand about)*

JULIAN

Oh, we've had a most . . . unusual . . .

LAWYER
(To BUTLER, *ignoring* JULIAN'S *answer)*

You've offered our guest refreshments?

JULIAN

Brother Julian.

BUTLER

Ice water, iced tea, and coffee—hot assumed, I imagine
—none taken.

LAWYER

Gracious! *(Back to* JULIAN*)* Port, perhaps. Removed people take port, I've noticed.

JULIAN
(More to please than anything)

Yes. Port. Please.

LAWYER *(To* BUTLER*)*

Port for . . .

JULIAN

Julian—Brother Julian.

LAWYER *(Slightly patronizing)*

I *know.* (BUTLER *goes to a sideboard)* I would join you,
but it is not my habit to drink before sundown. Not a
condemnation, you understand. One of my minor dis-
ciplines.

BUTLER
(Generally, looking at the bottle)

The port is eighteen-oh-six. *(To the* LAWYER*)* How do
they fortify wines, again?

JULIAN

Alcohol is added, more alcohol . . . at the time of cask-
ing. Fortify . . . strengthen.

BUTLER

Ah, yes.

LAWYER *(To* JULIAN*)*

Of course, your grandfather was a vintner, was he not.

JULIAN

Goodness, you . . . you have my history.

LAWYER

Oh, we do. Such a mild life . . . save those six years in
your thirties which are . . . blank . . . in our report
on you.

JULIAN
(A good covering laugh)

Oh, they were . . . mild, in their own way. Blank, but
not black.

LAWYER

Will you fill them for us? The blank years?

JULIAN
(Taking the glass from BUTLER*)*

Thank you. *(The laugh again)* They were nothing.

LAWYER *(Steelier)*

Still, you will fill them for us.

JULIAN
(Pleasant, but very firm)

No.

BUTLER

Gracious!

LAWYER

Recalcitrance, yes . . . well, we must have our people
dig further.

JULIAN

You'll find nothing interesting. You'll find some . . . up-
heaval, but . . . waste, mostly. Dull waste.

LAWYER

The look of most of our vices in retrospect, eh?

BUTLER *(Light)*

I have fleshpot visions: carousals, thighs and heavy perfume. . . .

LAWYER *(To* BUTLER*)*

It's in your mind, fitting, a mind worthy of your name.
(To JULIAN*)* Did you two . . . did he tell you his name,
and did you two have a veritable badminton over it?
Puns and chuckles?

JULIAN

We . . . labored it a bit, I more than . . . Butler, it
would appear.

BUTLER

I was churlish, I'm sorry. If there weren't so many of
you and only one of *me* . . .

JULIAN

Oh, now . . .

LAWYER *(Still on it)*

You're not going to tell me about those six years, eh?

JULIAN
*(Stares at him for a moment, then says it clear-
ly, enunciating)*
No.

(LAWYER shrugs)

BUTLER
May I have some port?

LAWYER *(Slightly incredulous)*
Do you *like* port?

BUTLER
Not very, but I thought I'd keep him company while you
play police.

LAWYER *(Shrugs again)*
It's not my house. *(Turns to* JULIAN*)* One can't say, "It's
not my castle," can one? *(Back to* BUTLER*)* If you think
it's proper.

BUTLER *(Getting himself some)*
Well, with the wine cellar stacked like a munitions dump,
and you "never having any" until the barn swallows start
screeping around . . .

LAWYER
There's no such word as screep.

BUTLER *(Shrugs)*
Fit.

JULIAN
I think it has a nice onomatopoetic ring about it . . .

LAWYER
(Down to business, rather rudely)
Your buddy told you why we sent for you?

JULIAN
(Offended, but pretending confusion)
My . . . buddy?

LAWYER
Mine, really. We were at school together. Did he tell you
that? *(As* JULIAN *intentionally looks blank)* His Eminence.

JULIAN
Ah!

LAWYER *(Imitation)*
Ah! *(Snapped)* Well? Did he?

JULIAN
(Choosing his words carefully, precisely)
His Eminence informed me . . . generally. He called me
into his . . .

LAWYER
. . . garden . . .

JULIAN
. . . garden . . . which is a comfortable office in summer . . .

BUTLER
Ninety-six today.

JULIAN *(Interested)*
Indeed!

BUTLER
More tomorrow.

LAWYER *(Impatiently)*
Called you into his garden.

JULIAN

And—sorry—and . . . told me of the high honor which
he had chosen for me.

LAWYER *(Scoffing)*

He. Chosen. You.

JULIAN

Of . . . your lady's most . . .

LAWYER

Miss Alice.

JULIAN

Of Miss Alice's—sorry, I've not met the lady yet, and
first names—of her overwhelming bequest to the
Church . . .

LAWYER

Not a bequest; a bequest is made in a will; Miss Alice is
not dead.

JULIAN

Uh . . . grant?

LAWYER

Grant.

JULIAN *(Taking a deep breath)*

Of her overwhelming grant to the Church, and of my
assignment to come here, to take care of . . .

LAWYER

Odds and ends.

JULIAN *(Shrugs one shoulder)*

. . . if you like. "A few questions and answers" was how
it was put to me.

BUTLER
(To LAWYER, *impressed)*

He's a lay brother.

LAWYER *(Bored)*

We *know. (For* JULIAN'S *benefit)* His Eminence—
buddy . . .

JULIAN *(Natural, sincere)*

Tch-tch-tch-tch-tch . . .

LAWYER

He was my buddy at school . . . if you don't mind.
(Beginning, now, to BUTLER, *but quickly becoming general)* His Eminence—though you have never met him,
Butler, seen him, perhaps—is a most . . . eminent man;
and bold, very bold; behind—or, underneath—what
would seem to be a solid rock of . . . pomposity, sham,
peacocking, there is a . . . flows a secret river . . .
of . . .

BUTLER *(For* JULIAN'S *benefit)*

This is an endless metaphor.

LAWYER

. . . of unconventionality, defiance, even. Simple sen-
tences? Is that all you want? Did you know that Brother
Julian here is the only lay brother in the history of Chris-
tendom assigned, chosen, as secretary and confidant to a
Prince of the Church? Ever?

JULIAN *(Mildly)*

That is not known as fact.

LAWYER

Name others!

JULIAN

I say it is not known as fact. I grant it is not usual—my
appointment as secretary to His Eminence. . . .

LAWYER *(Faint disgust)*

An honor, at any rate, an unusual honor for a lay
brother, an honor accorded by a most unusual Prince of
the Church—a prince of a man, in fact—a prince whose
still waters . . . well, you finish it.

BUTLER
(Pretending puzzlement as to how to finish it)
. . . whose still waters . . .

JULIAN

His Eminence is, indeed, a most unusual man.

LAWYER *(Sourly)*

I said he was a prince.

BUTLER
(Pretending to be talking to himself)
. . . run quiet? Run deep? Run *deep! That's* good!

LAWYER

Weren't there a few eyebrows raised at your appointment?

JULIAN

There . . . I was not informed of it . . . if there were.
His Eminence would not burden me. . . .

LAWYER
(Still to JULIAN, *patronizing)*
He is really Santa Claus; we know.

JULIAN *(Rising to it)*

Your animosity toward His Eminence must make your task very difficult for you. I must say I . . .

LAWYER

I have learned . . . *(Brief pause before he says the name with some distaste)* Brother Julian . . . never to confuse the representative of a . . . thing with the thing itself.

BUTLER

. . . though I wonder if you'd intended to get involved in *two* watery metaphors there: underground river, and still waters.

LAWYER *(To* BUTLER*)*

No, I had not. *(Back to* JULIAN*)* A thing with its representative. Your Cardinal and I loathe one another, and I find him unworthy of contempt. *(A hand up to stop any coming objection)* A cynic and a hypocrite, a posturer, but all the same the representative of an august and revered . . . body.

JULIAN *(Murmured)*

You are most unjust.

LAWYER
(As if he were continuing a prepared speech)

Uh . . . revered body. And Rome, in its perhaps wily—though *certainly* inscrutable—wisdom, Rome has found reason to appoint that wreckage as its representative.

JULIAN

Really, I can't permit you to talk that way.

LAWYER

You will permit it, you're under instructions, you have a

job to do. In fact, you have this present job be*cause* I
cannot stand your Cardinal.

JULIAN

He . . . he did not tell me so.

LAWYER

We tell you so.
(JULIAN *dips his head to one side in a "perhaps
it is true" gesture*)
And it is so.

JULIAN

I will not. . . I will not concern myself with . . . all
this.

BUTLER *(Quite to himself)*

I don't *like* port.

LAWYER *(To* BUTLER*)*

Then don't drink it. *(To* JULIAN*)* You're quite right: bow
your head, stop up your ears and do what you're told.

JULIAN

Obedience is not a fault.

LAWYER

Nor always a virtue. See Fascism.

JULIAN *(Rather strong for him)*

Perhaps we can get on with our business. . . .

LAWYER *(He, too)*

You don't want to take up my time, or your own.

JULIAN

Yes.

BUTLER *(Putting down glass)*
Then I won't drink it.

LAWYER
(To JULIAN, briskly, as to a servant)
All right! I shall tell Miss Alice you've come—that the
drab fledgling is pecking away in the library, impatient
for . . . food for the Church.

JULIAN
(A tight smile, a tiny formal bow)
If you would be so kind.

LAWYER *(Twisting the knife)*
I'll find out if she cares to see you today.

JULIAN *(Ibid.)*
Please.

LAWYER
(Moving toward the archway)
And, if she cares to, I will have you brought up.

JULIAN
(Mild surprise, but not a question)
Up.

LAWYER
(Almost challenging him)
Up. *(Pause)* You will not tell us about the six years—
those years blank but not black . . . the waste, the dull
waste.

JULIAN *(Small smile)*
No.

LAWYER *(He, too)*

You will . . . in time. *(To* BUTLER*)* Won't he, Butler?
Time? The great revealer?
*(*LAWYER *exits)*

JULIAN
(After the LAWYER *is gone; no indignation)*

Well.

BUTLER *(Offhand)*

Nasty man.

JULIAN
(Intentionally feigning surprise)

Oh? *(*HE *and* BUTLER *laugh)* Up.

BUTLER

Sir?

JULIAN

Up.

BUTLER

Oh! Yes! She . . . *(Moves to the model)* has her apart-
ments up . . . here. *(He points to a tower area)* Here.

JULIAN

A-ha.

BUTLER
(Straightening things up)

About those six years . . .

JULIAN
(Not unfriendly, very matter-of-fact)

What of them?

BUTLER

Yes, what of them?

JULIAN

Oh . . . *(Pause)* I . . . I lost my faith. *(Pause)* In God.

BUTLER

Ah. *(Then a questioning look)*

JULIAN

Is there more?

BUTLER

Is there more?

JULIAN

Well, nothing . . . of matter. I . . . declined. I . . . shriveled into myself; a glass dome . . . descended, and it seemed I was out of reach, unreachable, finally unreaching, in this . . . paralysis, of sorts. I . . . put myself in a mental home.

BUTLER
(Curiously noncommittal)

Ah.

JULIAN

I could not reconcile myself to the chasm between the nature of God and the use to which men put . . . God.

BUTLER

Between your God and others', your view and theirs.

JULIAN

I said what I intended: *(Weighs the opposites in each hand)* It is God the mover, not God the puppet; God the creator, not the God created by man.

BUTLER *(Almost pitying)*
Six years in the loony bin for semantics?

JULIAN
(Slightly flustered, heat)
It is not semantics! Men create a false God in their own image, it is easier for them! . . . It is not . . .

BUTLER
Levity! Forget it!

JULIAN
I . . . yes.
(A chime sounds)

BUTLER
Miss Alice will see you. I will take you up.

JULIAN
Forgive me . . . I . . .

BUTLER
(Moves toward archway)
Let me show you up.

JULIAN
You *did* ask me.

BUTLER *(Level)*
Yes, and you told me.

JULIAN
(An explanation, not an apology)
My faith and my sanity . . . they are one and the same.

BUTLER
Yes? *(Considers it)* A-ha. *(Smiles noncommittally)* We must not keep the lady waiting.
(They begin exiting, BUTLER *preceding* JULIAN)

CURTAIN

Scene Three

(An upstairs sitting room of the castle. Feminine, but not frilly. Blues instead of pinks. Fireplace in keeping with the castle. A door to the bedroom in the rear wall, stage left; a door from the hallway in the side wall, stage left. At rise, MISS ALICE is seated in a wing chair, facing windows, its back to the audience; the LAWYER is to one side, facing her)

LAWYER
(Pause, he has finished one sentence, is pondering another)
. . . Nor is it as simple as all that. The instinct of giving may die out in our time—if you'll grant that giving is an instinct. The government is far more interested in taking, in regulated taking, than in promoting spontaneous generosity. Remember what I told you—what we discussed—in reference to the charitable foundations, and how . . . *(A knock on the hall door)* That will be our bird of prey. Pray. P-R-A-Y. What a pun I could make on that; bird of pray. Come in.
(The hall door opens; BUTLER precedes JULIAN into the room)

BUTLER
Brother Julian, who *was* in the library, is now here.

LAWYER
So he is. *(To JULIAN, impatiently) Come* in, *come* in.

JULIAN *(Advancing a little)*
Yes . . . certainly.

BUTLER
May I go? I'm tired.

LAWYER *(Grandly)*
By all means.

BUTLER *(Turns to go)*
Thank you. *(To* JULIAN*)* Goodbye.

JULIAN
Goodb . . . I'll . . . we'll see one another again?

BUTLER
Oh. Yes, probably. *(As he exits)* Goodbye, everybody.

LAWYER
(After BUTLER *exits, chuckles)*
What is it the nouveaux riches are always saying? "You
can't get good servants nowadays"?

JULIAN
He seems . . .

LAWYER *(Curt)*
He is very good. *(Turns to the chair)* Miss Alice, our
Brother Julian is here. *(Repeats it, louder)* OUR BROTHER
JULIAN IS HERE. *(To* JULIAN*)* She's terribly hard of hear-
ing. *(To* MISS ALICE*)* DO YOU WANT TO SEE HIM? *(To*
JULIAN*)* I think she's responding. Sometimes . . . well,
at her age and condition . . . twenty minutes can go by
. . . for her to assimilate a sentence and reply to it.

JULIAN
But I thought . . . His Eminence said she was . . .
young.

LAWYER
SHHHHHHHH! She's moving.
     *(*MISS ALICE *slowly rises from her chair and
     comes around it. Her face is that of a withered*

crone, her hair gray and white and matted; she is bent; she moves with two canes)

MISS ALICE
(Finally, with a cracked and ancient voice, to JULIAN*)*
Hello there, young man.

LAWYER
(As JULIAN *takes a step forward)*
Hah! Don't come too close, you'll unnerve her.

JULIAN
But I'm terribly puzzled. I was led to believe that she was a young woman, and . . .

MISS ALICE
Hello there, young man.

LAWYER
Speak to her.

JULIAN
Miss . . . Miss Alice, how do you do?

LAWYER
Louder.

JULIAN
HOW DO YOU DO?

MISS ALICE *(To* LAWYER*)*
How do I do *what*?

LAWYER
It's a formality.

                    MISS ALICE
WHAT!?

                    LAWYER
IT IS A FORMALITY, AN OPENING GAMBIT.

                    MISS ALICE
Oh. *(To* JULIAN*)* How do *you* do?

                    JULIAN
Very well . . . thank you.

                    MISS ALICE
WHAT!?

                    JULIAN
VERY WELL, THANK YOU.

                    MISS ALICE
Don't you scream at me!

                    JULIAN *(Mumbled)*
Sorry.

                    MISS ALICE
WHAT!?

                    JULIAN
SORRY!

                    MISS ALICE *(Almost a pout)*
Oh.

                    LAWYER *(Who has enjoyed this)*
Well, I think I'll leave you two now . . . for your business. I'm sure you'll have a . . .

JULIAN
(An attempted urgent aside to the LAWYER*)*
Do you think you . . . shouldn't you be here? You've
. . . you've had more experience with her, and . . .

LAWYER *(Laughing)*
No, no, you'll get along fine. *(To* MISS ALICE*)* I'LL LEAVE
YOU TWO TOGETHER NOW. *(*MISS ALICE *nods vigorously)*
HIS NAME IS BROTHER JULIAN, AND THERE ARE SIX YEARS
MISSING FROM HIS LIFE. *(She nods again)* I'LL BE DOWN-
STAIRS. *(Begins to leave)*

MISS ALICE
(When the LAWYER *is at the door)*
Don't steal anything.

LAWYER *(Exiting)*
ALL RIGHT!

JULIAN
*(After a pause, begins bravely, taking a step for-
ward)*
Perhaps you should sit down. Let me . . .

MISS ALICE
WHAT!?

JULIAN
PERHAPS YOU SHOULD SIT DOWN!

MISS ALICE
(Not fear; malevolence)
Keep away from me!

JULIAN
Sorry. *(To himself)* Oh, really, this is impossible.

MISS ALICE
WHAT!?

JULIAN

I SAID THIS WAS IMPOSSIBLE.

MISS ALICE
(Thinks about that for a moment, then)
If you're a defrocked priest, what're you doing in all
that? *(Pointing to* JULIAN'S *garb)*

JULIAN

I AM NOT A DEFROCKED PRIEST, I AM A LAY BROTHER.
I HAVE NEVER BEEN A PRIEST.

MISS ALICE
What did you drink downstairs?

JULIAN
I had a glass of port . . . PORT!

MISS ALICE
(A spoiled, crafty child)
You didn't bring *me* one.

JULIAN
I had no idea you . . .

MISS ALICE
WHAT!?

JULIAN
SHALL I GET YOU A GLASS?

MISS ALICE
A glass of *what.*

JULIAN
PORT. A GLASS OF PORT.

MISS ALICE
(As if he were crazy)
What for?

JULIAN
BECAUSE YOU . . . *(To himself again)* Really, this *won't*
do.

MISS ALICE
*(Straightening up, ridding herself of the canes,
assuming a normal voice)*
I agree with you, it won't do, really.

JULIAN *(Astonishment)*
I beg your pardon?

MISS ALICE
I said it won't do at all.
*(SHE unfastens and removes her wig, unties and
takes off her mask, becomes herself, as JULIAN
watches, openmouthed)*
There. Is that better? And you needn't yell at me any
more; if anything, my hearing is *too* good.

JULIAN *(Slightly put out)*
I . . . I don't understand.

MISS ALICE
Are you annoyed?

JULIAN
I suspect I will be . . . might be . . . after the surprise
leaves me.

MISS ALICE *(Smiling)*
Don't be; it's only a little game.

JULIAN
Yes, doubtless. But why?

MISS ALICE
Oh, indulge us, please.

JULIAN
Well, of course, it would be my pleasure . . . but, considering the importance of our meeting . . .

MISS ALICE
Exactly. Considering the importance of our meeting.

JULIAN
A . . . a test for me.

MISS ALICE *(Laughs)*
No, not at all, a little lightness to counter the weight. *(Mock seriousness)* For we are involved in weighty matters . . . the transfer of millions, the rocking of empires. *(Normal, light tone again)* Let's be comfortable, shall we? Swing my chair around. *(JULIAN moves to do so)* As you can see—you *can,* I trust—I'm *not* a hundred and thirteen years old, but I *do* have my crotchets, even now: I have chairs everywhere that are mine—in each room . . . a chair that is mine, that I alone use.

JULIAN *(Moving the chair)*
Where would you . . .

MISS ALICE *(Lightly)*
Just . . . swing it . . . around. You needn't move it. Good. Now, sit with me. *(They sit)* Fine. In the dining room, of course, there is no question—I sit at the head of the table. But, in the drawing rooms, or the library, or whatever room you wish to mention, I have a chair that I consider my possession.

JULIAN

But you possess the entire . . . *(Thinks of a word)*
establishment.

MISS ALICE

Of course, but it is such a large . . . establishment that
one needs the feel of specific possession in every . . .
area.

JULIAN
(Rather shy, but pleasant)

Do you become . . . cross if someone accidentally assumes your chair, one of your chairs?

MISS ALICE
(Thinks about it, then)

How odd! Curiously, it has never happened, so I cannot
say. Tell me about yourself.

JULIAN

Well, there isn't much to say . . . much that isn't already known. Your lawyer would seem to have assembled
a case book on me, and . . .

MISS ALICE

Yes, yes, but not the things that would interest him, the
things that would interest me.

JULIAN *(Genuine interest)*

And what are they?

MISS ALICE *(Laughs again)*

Let me see. Ah! Do I terrify you?

JULIAN

You *did,* and you are still . . . awesome.

MISS ALICE *(Sweetly)*
Thank you. Did my lawyer intimidate you?

JULIAN
It would seem to be his nature—or his pleasure—to intimidate, and . . . well, I am, perhaps, more easily intimidated than some.

MISS ALICE
Perhaps you are, but he *is* a professional. And how did you find Butler?

JULIAN
A gentle man, quick . . . but mostly gentle.

MISS ALICE
Gentle, yes. He was my lover at one time. *(As* JULIAN *averts his head)* Oh! Perhaps I shouldn't have told you.

JULIAN
No, forgive me. Things sometimes . . . are so unexpected.

MISS ALICE
Yes, they are. I am presently mistress to my lawyer—the gentleman who intimidated you so. He is a pig.

JULIAN *(Embarrassed)*
Yes, yes. You have . . . never married.

MISS ALICE *(Quiet amusement)*
Alas.

JULIAN
You are . . . not Catholic.

MISS ALICE *(The same)*
Again, alas.

JULIAN

No, it is fortunate you are not.

MISS ALICE

I am bored with my present lover.

JULIAN

I . . . *(Shrugs)*

MISS ALICE

I was not soliciting advice.

JULIAN *(Quiet laugh)*

Good, for I have none.

MISS ALICE

These six years of yours.

JULIAN

(Says it all in one deep breath)

There is no mystery to it, my faith in God left me, and
I committed myself to an asylum. *(Pause)* You see?
Nothing to it.

MISS ALICE

What an odd place to go to look for one's faith.

JULIAN

You misunderstand me. I did not go there to *look* for
my faith, but because *it* had left me.

MISS ALICE

You tell it so easily.

JULIAN *(Shrugs)*

It is easy to tell.

MISS ALICE

Ah.

JULIAN *(Giggles a little)*

However, I would not tell your present . . . uh, your lawyer. And that made him quite angry.

MISS ALICE

Have you slept with many women?

JULIAN *(Carefully)*

I am not certain.

MISS ALICE *(Tiny laugh)*

It is an easy enough thing to determine.

JULIAN

Not so. For one, I am celibate. A lay brother—you must know—while not a priest, while not ordained, is still required to take vows. And chastity is one of them.

MISS ALICE

A dedicated gesture, to be sure, celibacy without priesthood . . . but a melancholy one, for you're a handsome man . . . in your way.

JULIAN

You're kind.

MISS ALICE

But, tell me: why did you not become a priest? Having gone so far, I should think . . .

JULIAN

A lay brother serves.

MISS ALICE

. . . but is not ordained, is more a servant.

JULIAN

The house of God is so grand . . . *(Sweet apologetic smile)* it needs many servants.

MISS ALICE

How humble. But is that the only reason?

JULIAN

I am not wholly reconciled. Man's God and mine are not . . . close friends.

MISS ALICE

Indeed. But, tell me, how are you not certain that you have slept with a woman?

JULIAN *(With curiosity)*

Shall I tell you? We have many more important matters . . . .

MISS ALICE

Tell me, please. The money will not run off. Great wealth is patient.

JULIAN

I would not know. Very well. It's good for me, I think, to talk about it. The institution . . . to which I committed myself—it was deep inland, by the way—was a good one, good enough, and had, as I am told most do, sections— buildings, or floors of buildings—for patients in various conditions . . . some for violent cases, for example, others for children. . . .

MISS ALICE

How sad.

JULIAN

Yes. Well, at any rate . . . sections. Mine . . . my section was for people who were . . . mildly troubled—

which I found ironic, for I have never considered the flee-
ing of faith a mild matter. Nonetheless, for the mildly
troubled. The windows were not barred; one was allowed
utensils, and one's own clothes. You see, escape was not
a matter of urgency, for it was a section for mildly
troubled people who had committed themselves, and
should escape occur, it was not a danger for the world
outside.

MISS ALICE

I understand.

JULIAN

There was a period during my stay, however, when I
began to . . . hallucinate, and to withdraw, to a point
where I was not entirely certain when my mind was
tricking me, or when it was not. I believe one would say
—how is it said?—that my grasp on reality was . . .
tenuous—occasionally. There was, at the same time, in
my section, a woman who, on very infrequent occasions,
believed that she was the Virgin Mary.

MISS ALICE (Mild surprise)

My goodness.

JULIAN

A quiet woman, plain, but soft features, not hard; at
forty, or a year either side, married, her husband the
owner of a dry-goods store, if my memory is correct;
childless . . . the sort of woman, in short, that one is
not aware of passing on the street, or in a hallway . . .
unlike you—if you will permit me.

MISS ALICE (Smiles)

It may be I am . . . noticeable, but almost never identi-
fied.

JULIAN

You shun publicity.

MISS ALICE

Oh, indeed. And I have few friends . . . that, too, by choice. *(Urges him on with a gesture)* But please . . .

JULIAN

Of course. My hallucinations . . . were saddening to me. I suspect I should have been frightened of them—as well as by them—most people are, or would be . . . by hallucinations. But I was . . . saddened. They were, after all, provoked, brought on by the departure of my faith, and this in turn was brought on by the manner in which people mock God. . . .

MISS ALICE

I notice you do not say you lost your faith, but that it abandoned you.

JULIAN

Do I. Perhaps at bottom I had lost it, but I think more that I was confused . . . *and* intimidated . . . by the world about me, and let slip contact with it . . . with my faith. So, I was *sad*dened.

MISS ALICE

Yes.

JULIAN

The periods of hallucination would be announced by a ringing in the ears, which produced, or was accompanied by, a loss of hearing. I would hear people's voices from a great distance and through the roaring of . . . surf. And my body would feel light, and not mine, and I would float—no, glide.

MISS ALICE

There was no feeling of terror in this? I would be beside myself.

JULIAN

No, as I said, sadness. Aaaaahhh, I would think, I am going from myself again. How very, very sad . . . everything. Loss, great loss.

MISS ALICE

I understand.

JULIAN

And when I was away from myself—never far enough, you know, to . . . blank, just to . . . fog over—when I was away from myself I could not sort out my imaginings from what was real. Oh, sometimes I would say to a nurse or one of the attendants, "Could you tell me, did I preach last night? To the patients? A fire-and-brimstone lesson. Did I do that, or did I imagine it?" And they would tell me, if they knew.

MISS ALICE

And did you?

JULIAN

Hm? . . . No, it would seem I did not . . . to their knowledge. But I was never sure, you see.

MISS ALICE (Nodding)

No.

JULIAN (A brief, rueful laugh)

I imagined so many things, or . . . did so many things I thought I had imagined. The uncertainty . . . you know?

MISS ALICE (Smiles)

Are you sure you're not describing what passes for sanity?

JULIAN
(Laughs briefly, ruefully)

Perhaps. But one night . . . now, there! You see? I said
"one night," and I'm not sure, even now, whether or not
this thing happened or, if it did not happen, it did or did
not happen at noon, or in the morning, much less at night
. . . yet I say night. Doubtless one will do as well as
another. So. One *night* the following either happened or
did not happen. I was walking in the gardens—or I imagined I was walking in the gardens—walking in the gardens, and I heard a sound . . . sounds from near where
a small pool stood, with rosebushes, rather overgrown, a
formal garden once, the . . . the place had been an
estate, I remember being told. Sounds . . . sobbing?
Low cries. And there was, as well, the ringing in my
ears, and . . . and fog, a . . . a milkiness, between myself and . . . everything. I went toward the cries, the
sounds, and . . . I, I fear my description will become
rather . . . vivid now. . . .

MISS ALICE
I am a grown woman.

JULIAN *(Nods)*
Yes. *(A deep breath)* The . . . the woman, the woman
I told you about, who hallucinated, herself, that she was
the Virgin . . .

MISS ALICE
Yes, yes.

JULIAN
. . . was . . . was on a grassy space by the pool—or
this is what I imagined—on the ground, and she was in
her . . . a nightdress, a . . . gossamer, filmy thing, or
perhaps she was not, but there she was, on the ground,
on an incline, a slight incline, and when she saw me—or

sensed me there—she raised her head, and put her arms
. . . (*Demonstrates*) . . . out, in a . . . supplication,
and cried, "Help me, help me . . . help me, oh God,
God, help me . . . oh, help, help." This, over and over,
and with the sounds in her throat between. I . . . I came
closer, and the sounds, her sounds, her words, the roaring
in my ears, the gossamer and the milk film, I . . . a
ROAR, AN OCEAN! Saliva, perfume, sweat, the taste of
blood and rich earth in the mouth, sweet sweaty slipping
. . . (*Looks to her apologetically, nods*) . . . ejacula-
tion. (*She nods*) The sound cascading away, the rhythms
breaking, everything slowly, limpid, quieter, damper, soft
. . . soft, quiet . . . done.

> *They are both silent.* MISS ALICE *is gripping the
> arms of her chair;* JULIAN *continues softly*)

I have described it to you, as best I can, as it . . . happened, or did not happen.

MISS ALICE
(*Curiously . . . dispassionately*)
I . . . am a very beautiful woman.

JULIAN
*After a pause which serves as reply to her
statement*)
I must tell you more, though. You *have* asked me for an
entirety.

MISS ALICE
And a very rich one.

JULIAN (*Brief pause, nods*)
As I mentioned to you, the woman was given to hallucinations as well, but perhaps I should have said that being the
Virgin Mary was merely the strongest of her . . . delu-
sions; she . . . hallucinated . . . as well as the next
person, about perfectly mundane matters, too. So it may

be that now we come to coincidence, or it may not. Shortly—several days—after the encounter I have described to you—the encounter which did or did not happen—the woman . . . I do not know which word to use here, either descended or ascended into an ecstasy, the substance of which was that she was with child . . . that she was pregnant with the Son of God.

MISS ALICE

And I live here, in all these rooms.

JULIAN

You don't laugh? Well, perhaps you will, at *me*. I was . . . beside myself, for I assumed the piling of delusion upon delusion, though the chance of there being fact, happening, there somewhere . . . I went to my . . . doctor and told him of my hallucination—if indeed that is what it was. He told me, then . . . that the woman had been examined, that she was suffering from cancer of the womb, that it was advanced, had spread. In a month, she died.

MISS ALICE

Did you believe it?

JULIAN *(Small smile)*

That she died?

MISS ALICE

That you spoke with your doctor.

JULIAN *(Pause)*

It has never occurred to me until this moment to doubt it. He has informed me many times.

MISS ALICE

Ah?

JULIAN

I *do see* him . . . in reality. We have become friends,
we talk from time to time. Socially.

MISS ALICE

Ah. And was it he who discharged you from . . . your
asylum?

JULIAN

I was persuaded, eventually, that perhaps I was . . .
overconcerned by hallucination; that some was inevitable,
and a portion of that—even desirable.

MISS ALICE

Of course.

JULIAN *(Looking at his hands)*

Have I answered your question? That I am not . . . sure
that I have slept with a woman.

MISS ALICE
(Puzzling . . . slowly)

I don't . . . know. Is the memory of something having
happened the same as it having happened?

JULIAN

It is not the nicest of . . . occurrences—to have described to you.

MISS ALICE *(Kindly)*

It was many years ago. *(Then, an afterthought)* Was it
not?

JULIAN

Yes, yes, quite a while ago.

MISS ALICE *(Vaguely amused)*
I am rich and I am beautiful and I live here in all these
rooms . . . without relatives, with a . . . *(Wry)* com-
panion, from time to time . . . *(Leans forward, whispers,
but still amused)* . . . and with a secret.

JULIAN
Oh? *(Trying to be light, too)* And may I know it? The
secret?

MISS ALICE
I don't know yet.

JULIAN *(Relaxing)*
Ah-ha.

MISS ALICE
(Sudden change of mood, to brisk, official, cool)
Well then. You're here on business, not for idle conver-
sation, I believe.

JULIAN
(Confused, even a little hurt)
Oh . . . yes, that's . . . that's right.

MISS ALICE
You have instruction to give me—not formal, I'm not
about to settle in your faith. Information, facts, questions
and answers.

JULIAN *(Slightly sour)*
Odds and ends, I believe.

MISS ALICE *(Sharp)*
To you, perhaps. But important if you're to succeed, if
you're not to queer the whole business, if you're not
to . . .

JULIAN

Yes, yes!

MISS ALICE

So you'll be coming back here . . . when I wish to see
you.

JULIAN

Yes.

MISS ALICE

Several times. It might be better if you were to move in.
I'll decide it.

JULIAN

Oh . . . well, of course, if you think . . .

MISS ALICE

I think. (JULIAN *nods acquiescence*) Very good. (SHE
rises) No more today, no more now.

JULIAN
(Up, maybe retreating a little)
Well, if you'll let me know when . . .

MISS ALICE

Come here.
(JULIAN goes to her; she takes his head in her
hands, kisses him on the forehead, he registers
embarrassment, she laughs, a slightly mocking,
unnerving laugh)
Little recluse. *(Laughs again)*

JULIAN

If you'll . . . advise me, or His Eminence, when you'd
like me to . . .

MISS ALICE
Little bird, pecking away in the library. *(Laughs again)*

JULIAN
I'm . . . disappointed you find me so . . . humorous.

MISS ALICE
(Cheerful, but not contrite)
Oh, forgive me, I live so alone, the oddest things cheer
me up. You . . . cheer me up. *(Holds out her hand to
be kissed)* Here. *(*JULIAN *hesitates)* Ah-ah-ah, he who
hesitates loses all.
> *(*JULIAN *hesitates again, momentarily, then
> kisses her hand, but kneeling, as he would kiss
> a Cardinal's ring.* MISS ALICE *laughs at this)*
Do you think I am a Cardinal? Do I look like a Prince?
Have you never even kissed a woman's hand?

JULIAN
(Back on his feet, evenly)
No. I have not.

MISS ALICE *(Kindlier now)*
I'll send for you, we'll have . . . pleasant afternoons,
you and I. Goodbye.
> *(*MISS ALICE *turns away from* JULIAN, *gazes out
> a window, her back to the audience.* JULIAN
> exits. The* LAWYER *enters the set from the bed-
> room door)*

LAWYER
(To MISS ALICE, *a bit abruptly)*
How did it go, eh?

MISS ALICE
(Turns around, matter-of-factly)
Not badly.

LAWYER

You took long enough.

(MISS ALICE *shrugs*)

When are you having him again?

MISS ALICE *(Very wickedly)*

On business, or privately?

LAWYER

Don't be childish.

MISS ALICE

Whenever you like, whenever you say. *(Seriously)* Tell me honestly, do you really think we're wise?

LAWYER

Wise? Well, we'll see. If we prove not, I can't think of anything standing in the way that can't be destroyed. *(Pause)* Can you?

MISS ALICE *(Rather sadly)*

No. Nothing.

CURTAIN

ACT TWO

Scene One

(The library—as of Act One, Scene Two. No one on stage. Evening. MISS ALICE *hurtles through the archway, half running, half backing, with the* LAWYER *after her. It is not a chase; she has just broken from him, and her hurtling is the result of sudden freeing)*

MISS ALICE
(Just before and as she is entering; her tone is neither hysterical nor frightened; she is furious and has been mildly hurt)
KEEP . . . GO! GET YOUR . . . LET GO OF ME! *(She is in the room)* KEEP OFF! KEEP OFF ME!

LAWYER
(Excited, ruffled, but trying to maintain decorum)
Don't be hysterical, now.

MISS ALICE
(Still moving away from him, as he comes on)
KEEP . . . AWAY. JUST STAY AWAY FROM ME.

LAWYER
I said don't be hysterical.

MISS ALICE
I'll *show* you hysteria. I'll give you *fireworks!* KEEP! Keep away.

LAWYER
(Soothing, but always moving in on her)

A simple touch, an affectionate hand on you; nothing more . . .

MISS ALICE *(Quiet loathing)*
You're degenerate.

LAWYER *(Steely)*
An affectionate hand, in the privacy of a hallway . . .

MISS ALICE *(Almost a shriek)*
THERE ARE PEOPLE!!

LAWYER
Where? There are no people.

MISS ALICE *(Between her teeth)*
There are people.

LAWYER *(Feigning surprise)*
There are no people. *(To a child)* Ahh! *(Walks toward the model, indicates it)* Unless you mean all the little people running around inside here. Is that what you mean?

MISS ALICE
(A mirthless, don't-you-know-it laugh)
Hunh-hunh-hunh-hunh.

LAWYER
Is that who you mean? All the little people in here? *(Change of tone to normal, if sarcastic)* Why don't we show them a few of your tricks, hunh?

MISS ALICE
(Moving away, clenched teeth again)
Keep . . . away . . . from . . . me.

LAWYER *(Without affection)*

To love is to possess, and since I desire to possess you, that must mean conversely that I love you, must it not. Come here.

MISS ALICE *(With great force)*

PEOPLE!

LAWYER

Your little priest? Your little Julian? He is not. . .

MISS ALICE

He is not a priest!

LAWYER

No. And he is not nearby—momentarily! *(Hissed)* I am sick of him here day after day, sick of the time you're taking. Will you get it done with!

MISS ALICE

No! He will be *up.*

LAWYER

Oh, for Christ's sake, he's a connoisseur; he'll be nosing around the goddam wine cellar for hours!

MISS ALICE

He will be *up. (Afterthought)* Butler!

LAWYER *(Advancing)*

Butler? Let him watch. *(A sneer)* Which is something I've been meaning to discuss with you for the longest time now. . . .

MISS ALICE
(Calm, quivering hatred; almost laughing with it)
I have a loathing for you that I can't *describe.*

LAWYER

You were never one with words. *(Suddenly brutal)* NOW,
COME HERE.

MISS ALICE *(Shrugs)*

All right. I won't react, I promise you.

LAWYER
(Beginning to fondle her)

Won't react . . . indeed.
> *(During this next, MISS ALICE is backed up
> against something, and the LAWYER is calmly
> at her, kissing her neck, fondling her. She is
> calm, and at first he seems amused)*

MISS ALICE

What causes this loathing I have for you? It's the *way*
you have, I suppose; the clinical way; methodical,
slow . . .

LAWYER

. . . thorough . . .

MISS ALICE

. . . uninvolved . . .

LAWYER

. . . oh, very involved . . .

MISS ALICE

. . . impersonality in the most personal things . . .

LAWYER

. . . your passivity is exciting . . .

MISS ALICE

. . . passive only to some people . . . *(He nips her)* ow.

LAWYER

A little passion; good.

MISS ALICE

*(As he continues fondling her; perhaps by the
end he has her dress off her shoulders)*

With so much . . . many things to loathe, I must choose
carefully, to impress you most with it.

LAWYER

Um-humh.

MISS ALICE

Is it the hair? Is it the hair on your back I loathe most?
Where the fat lies, on your shoulderblades, the hair on
your back . . . black, ugly? . . .

LAWYER

But too short to get a hold on, eh?

MISS ALICE

Is it that—the back hair? It could be; it would be enough.
Is it your . . . what is the polite word for it . . . your sex?

LAWYER *(Mocking)*

Careful now, with a man's pride.

MISS ALICE

Ugly; that too—ugly.

LAWYER *(Unruffled)*

Better than most, if you care for a *man* . . .

MISS ALICE

. . . ugly coarse uncut ragged . . . PUSH!

LAWYER

Push . . . yes . . .

MISS ALICE

. . . selfish, hurtful, ALWAYS! OVER AND OVER!

LAWYER

You like it; it feels good.

MISS ALICE
(Very calm and analytical)

But is that what I loathe most? It could be; that would be enough, too.

LAWYER

. . . oh, what a list . . .

MISS ALICE

But I think it is most the feel of your skin . . . *(Hard)* that you can't sweat. *(He stiffens some)* That your body is as impersonal as your . . . self—dry, uncaring, rubbery . . . dead. Ah . . . there . . . that is what I loathe about you most: you're dead. Moving pushing selfish dry dead. *(Brief pause)* Does that hurt? Does something finally, beautifully hurt? *(Self-mocking laugh)* Have I finally gotten . . . into you?

LAWYER
(A little away from her now)

Insensitive, still, aren't you, after all this time. Does it hurt? Does something finally hurt?

MISS ALICE

. . . deep, gouging hurt?

LAWYER

Everything! Everything in the day and night, eating, resting, walking, rutting, everything! Everything *hurts*.

MISS ALICE

Awwwwww.

LAWYER

Inside the . . . sensibility, everything hurts. Deeply.

MISS ALICE *(Ridiculing)*

And is that why I loathe you?

LAWYER *(A quiet, rueful laugh)*

Probably. *(Quickly back to himself)* But you, little play-mate, you're what I want now. GIVE!

MISS ALICE

If Julian comes in here . . .

LAWYER *(Shoves her)*

Are you playing it straight, hunh? Or do you like your work a little bit, hunh? *(Again)* Do you enjoy spreading your legs for the clergy? *(Again)* Hunh?

MISS ALICE

STOP! . . . YOU!

LAWYER

Is that our private donation to the Church? Our own grant? YES? *(Begins to hurt her arm)* Are we planning to turn into a charitable, educational foundation?

MISS ALICE *(In pain)*

My arm!

(BUTLER enters, unnoticed; watches)

LAWYER
(Hard and very serious)

Don't you dare mess this thing up. You behave the way I've told you; you PLAY-ACT. You do your part; STRAIGHT.

BUTLER *(Calmly)*

Brother Julian . . .

MISS ALICE

Butler! Help me!

BUTLER
(As the LAWYER *releases her)*
. . . has now examined the wine cellar, with awe and
much murmuring, and will be with us presently. He's
peeing. So I suggest—unless you're doing this for his
benefit—uh, you stop.

MISS ALICE
(As she and the LAWYER *pull themselves together)*
He hurt me, Butler.

BUTLER
(Calmly, as if reminding her)
Often. *(To the* LAWYER, *with mock friendliness)* Up to
your old tricks, eh?

LAWYER *(Dusting himself off)*
She is . . . not behaving.

BUTLER *(Very noncommittal)*
Ah me.

MISS ALICE
(Under her breath, to the LAWYER*)*
Savage! *(Realizes)* Both of you!

LAWYER *(Laughs)*
The maiden in the shark pond.

MISS ALICE
He thinks I'm sleeping with Julian. *(To* LAWYER*)* You
poor jealous . . .

BUTLER

Are you?

MISS ALICE *(Indignant)*
No! *(Almost sad about it)* No, I am not.

LAWYER
She is!

MISS ALICE
I said I am not!

BUTLER
Are you going to?

MISS ALICE
(After a pause; to LAWYER*)*
Am I going to? Am I going to . . . spread my legs for
the clergy? Enjoy my work a little? Isn't that what you'd
have me do? To not mess it up? To play my part straight?
Isn't that what you'll HAVE ME DO?

LAWYER
You don't need urging! . . .

BUTLER
Now, children . . .

MISS ALICE
When the time comes? Won't you have me at him? Like
it or not? Well. . . I will like it!
(A little hard breathing from MISS ALICE *and
the* LAWYER*)*

BUTLER
Something *should* be done about the wine cellar. I've
noticed it—as a passerby would—but Brother Julian
pointed out the extent of it to me: bottles have burst, are
bursting, corks rotting . . . something to do with the
temperature or the dampness. It's a shame, you know.

MISS ALICE *(Surprisingly shrill)*
Well, fix it!

BUTLER *(Ignoring her tone)*
Some great years, popping, dribbling away, going to vine-
gar under our feet. There is a Mouton Rothschild—one
I'm especially fond of—that's . . .

LAWYER *(Pacifying)*
Do. Do . . . fix it.

BUTLER *(Shakes his head)*
Going. All of it. Great shame.

LAWYER
Yes, yes.

BUTLER *(Brightly)*
Nice thing about having Julian here so much . . . he's
helpful. Wines, plants . . . do you know, he told me
some astonishing things about ferns. We were in the
solarium . . .

MISS ALICE *(Quiet pleading)*
Please . . . stop.

BUTLER
Oh. Well, it's nice having him about.

LAWYER *(Sour)*
Oh, we'll be a foursome very soon.

MISS ALICE *(Brightly)*
Yes.

LAWYER
(With a mirthless smile)
Warning.

BUTLER *(Cheerful again)*

It *would* be a great deal more sensible than . . . puttering out here every day. We could put him over the chapel! Now, that's a splendid idea. He likes the chapel, he said, not resonant, too small or something, wrong angles, but he likes it . . .

MISS ALICE

When he moves here . . .

LAWYER

He will move here when I say—and as I say.

MISS ALICE *(Fake smile)*

We shall see.

LAWYER *(Still offhand)*

We shall not see.

JULIAN *(Offstage)*

Halloo!

BUTLER

In . . . in here.

MISS ALICE
(Sotto voce to the LAWYER*)*

You say we shall not see? *Shall* we?

LAWYER *(As above)*

Warning.

*(*JULIAN *enters)*
JULIAN

Ah! There you all are.

LAWYER
We had wondered where *you* were.

MISS ALICE *(Reminding a child)*
You usually find us here after dinner.

JULIAN
Yes, and a superb dinner.

LAWYER
. . . and then Butler reminded us that you were in the
cellar.

JULIAN *(Sincere, but prepared)*
Miss Alice, your . . . home possesses two things that,
were I a designer of houses—for the very wealthy, of
course—I would put in all my designs.

MISS ALICE *(Smiling)*
And what are they?

LAWYER
(To MISS ALICE, *mildly mocking* JULIAN*)*
Can't you guess?

MISS ALICE *(Charmingly)*
Of course I can guess, but I want Julian to have the
pleasure of saying it.

JULIAN
A chapel and a wine cellar.

MISS ALICE
(Agreeing, but is she making light fun?)
Yes.

LAWYER
We hear, though, that the wine cellar is a wreck. And
aren't there cobwebs in the chapel, too?

JULIAN
(Light but standing up to him)
One or two spiders have been busy around the altar, and
the organ is . . . in need of use . . .

LAWYER *(Very funny to him)*
HUNH!

JULIAN *(Choosing to ignore it)*
. . . but it *is* a chapel, a good one. The wine cellar, however . . . *(Shakes his head)* . . . great, great shame.

BUTLER
Exactly my words.

MISS ALICE
Well, we must have it tended to—and especially since
you are our guest so frequently these days, and enjoy
good wines.

JULIAN
I would call someone in, a specialist, if I were you.

LAWYER *(Patronizing)*
Why? Can't you take care of it? Your domain?

JULIAN *(Quietly)*
The chapel, more, I should think.

BUTLER
Where does the Church get its wine . . . for Communion
and the like?

JULIAN

Oh, it is grown, *made* . . . grown, the grapes, harvested,
pressed . . . by, by monks.

LAWYER *(False heartiness)*

A regular profit-making setup, the Church.

JULIAN *(Quietly, as usual)*

Self-sustaining . . . in some areas.

LAWYER

But not in others, eh? Sometimes the old beggar bell
comes out, doesn't it? Priest as leper.

MISS ALICE
(Mildly to the LAWYER)

It *is* true: you are not fit for God's sight.

BUTLER
(To the LAWYER; cheerfully interested)

Is that *so!* I wasn't sure.

LAWYER
(To MISS ALICE, feigning curiosity and surprise)

Who whispered it to you?

MISS ALICE
(Indicating JULIAN. Semi-serious)

My confessor.

LAWYER *(A sneer; to JULIAN)*

Did you? And so *you* object, as well? To my mention of
the Church as solicitor.

JULIAN

In England I believe *you* would be referred to as solicitor.

LAWYER

No, I would not. And we are not in England . . . are
we?

BUTLER

This *place* was . . . in England.

MISS ALICE
(As if suddenly remembering)
Yes, it was! Every stone, marked and shipped.

JULIAN

Oh; I had thought it was a replica.

LAWYER

Oh no; that would have been too simple. Though it *is* a
replica . . . in its way.

JULIAN

Of?

LAWYER
(Pointing to the model)
Of that.
        (JULIAN laughs a little; the LAWYER shrugs)
Ah well.

JULIAN *(To MISS ALICE)*

Did your . . . did your father have it . . . put up? *(A
parenthesis)* It suddenly occurred to me that I know nothing of your family, though I . . . I don't mean to
pry . . .

MISS ALICE *(A private laugh)*

No, we must not . . . well, should we say that? That my
father put it up? No. Let us not say that.

BUTLER

To JULIAN, *pointing first to the model, then to the room)*

Do you mean the model . . . or the replica?

JULIAN

I mean the . . . I mean . . . what we are in.

BUTLER

Ah-ha. And which is that?

JULIAN

That we are in?

BUTLER

Yes.

LAWYER *(To* JULIAN)

You are clearly not a Jesuit. *(Turning)* Butler, you've put him in a clumsy trap.

BUTLER *(Shrugging)*

I'm only a servant.

LAWYER

(To JULIAN, *too sweetly)*

You needn't accept his alternative . . . that since we are clearly not in a model we must be in a replica.

BUTLER *(Vaguely annoyed)*

Why must he not accept that?

MISS ALICE

Yes. Why not?

LAWYER

I said he did not *need* to accept the alternative. I did not say it was not valid.

JULIAN *(Cheerfully)*
I will not accept it; the problem is only semantic.

BUTLER
(Perhaps too consoling)
Well, yes; that's what I would have thought.

LAWYER
Not necessarily, though. Depends, doesn't it, on your con-
cept of reality, on the limit of possibilities. . . .

MISS ALICE *(Genuinely put off)*
Oh, Lord!

LAWYER
There are no limits to possibi . . . *(Suddenly embarrassed)* I'm . . . I'm sorry.

MISS ALICE
(To JULIAN, *but at the* LAWYER*)*
He starts in, he *will;* give him the most sophomoric conun-
drum, and he'll bore you to death.

LAWYER *(Violently)*
I! Will! Not!

JULIAN *(To break the silence)*
Well . . . perhaps I'm at fault here.

MISS ALICE *(Quietly, kindly)*
How could you be? . . . Dear Julian.

LAWYER
(To MISS ALICE*; burning)*
I thought I had educated you; I thought I had drilled you
sufficiently in matters of consequence; *(Growing louder)*
I thought I had made it clear to you the way you were to
behave.

JULIAN
Perhaps I should leave now; I think that . . .

LAWYER
DON'T INTERRUPT ME!
(Glares at JULIAN, *who moves off to the model)*

MISS ALICE
(To the LAWYER; *calmly)*
You forget your place.

LAWYER
(Clearly trying to get hold of himself)
I . . . you . . . are quite right . . . Miss Alice, and
abstractions *are* upsetting.

MISS ALICE
(To the LAWYER; *patiently)*
Perhaps you'll go home now.

BUTLER *(Cheerfully)*
Shall I have your car brought around?

LAWYER
(Trying to be private in public)
I . . . I thought that with so much to attend to, I might
. . . spend the night. Of course, if you'd rather I
didn't . . .
            (Leaves it unfinished. MISS ALICE *smiles
                    enigmatically)*

BUTLER
(Pretending to think the remark was for him)
I don't mind whether you do or not.

JULIAN
(Peering at the model, rather amazed)
Can it . . . can it be?

LAWYER
In the heat of . . . I, I forgot myself.

MISS ALICE
(Patronizingly sweet)
Yes.

LAWYER *(Matter-of-fact)*
You will forgive me.

MISS ALICE *(Toying)*
Oh?

BUTLER
Shall I have his car brought around?

LAWYER *(Sudden softening)*
Let me stay.

JULIAN
(Shy attempt at getting attention)
Please . . .

MISS ALICE
(Malicious pleasure in it)
I don't know . . .

JULIAN *(More urgently)*
Please!

LAWYER *(Bitter)*
As you wish, of course.
          *(Swings his hand back as if to strike her;
                    she flinches)*

JULIAN
PLEASE!

BUTLER
(Patiently amused curiosity)
What *is* it, for heaven's sake?

JULIAN *(Pointing to the model)*
The model is . . . on fire; it's on fire!

BUTLER
(Urgent dropping of butlerish attitudes)
Where!

LAWYER
Good Christ!

MISS ALICE
Quick!
(The LAWYER and BUTLER rush to the model)

BUTLER
Where, for Christ's sake!

JULIAN *(Jostled)*
In the . . . over the . . .

LAWYER
Find it!

BUTLER
*(Peering into various windows with great
agitation)*
It's . . . it's the . . . where the hell is it! . . . It's the
. . . chapel! The chapel's burning!

MISS ALICE
Hurry!

BUTLER
Come on! Let's get to it! *(Begins to run out of the room)*
Are you coming? Julian!

JULIAN
(Confused, but following)
But I . . . but . . . yes, of course.
(JULIAN and BUTLER run out)

MISS ALICE
(To the LAWYER as he hangs back)
We're burning down! Hurry!

LAWYER
*(Comes up to her, grabs her by the wrist, forces
her to the ground, keeps hold)*
Burning down? Consumed? WHY NOT! Remember what I
told you. Watch . . . your . . . step!
*(He runs out after the others. MISS ALICE is left
alone; maybe we hear one or two diminishing
shouts from the others, offstage. Finally, silence.
MISS ALICE doesn't rise from the floor, but
gradually assumes a more natural position
on it)*

MISS ALICE
*(She alternates between a kind of incantation-
prayer and a natural tone)*
(Prayer)
Let the fire be put out. Let the chapel be saved; let the
fire not spread; let us not be consumed.
(Natural)
He hurt me. My wrist hurts. Who was the boy when I
was little hurt my wrist? I don't remember.
(Prayer)
Let the fire not spread; let them be quick.
(Natural)
YOU PIG!
(Softly, almost a whine)
You hurt my wrist.

(Imitates the LAWYER'S *tone)*

Watch . . . your . . . step.

(Prayer)

Oh God, I have watched my step. I have . . . trod . . .
so carefully.

(Natural and weary)

Let it all come down—let the whole place . . . go.
*(She must now, when using a natural tone, al-
most give the suggestion of talking to someone
in the model. Natural)*

I don't mean that. I don't remember his name . . . or
his face; merely the hurt . . . and that continues, the
hurt the same, the name and the face changing, but it
doesn't matter. Let them save it.

(Prayer)

Let them save it. Don't . . . destroy. Let them save the
resonance.

(Natural)

Increase it. Julian says there is no resonance, that it's not
right.

(Prayer)

Let the resonance increase.

(Natural; a little-girl tone)

I have tried very hard to be careful, to obey, to withhold
my . . . nature? I have tried so hard to be good, but I'm
. . . such a stranger . . . here.

(Prayer)

I have tried to obey what I have not understood, understanding that I must obey. Don't destroy! I have tried!
TRIED.

(Natural)

Is that the way about hurt? That *it* does not change . . .
but merely its agents?

*(*JULIAN *appears, unseen by* MISS ALICE*)*

(Natural, still)

I will hold on.

(Sweetly, apologetically)

I will try to hold on.

(Prayer)

I will try to hold on!

(Natural)

Please, please . . . if you *do* . . . be generous and gentle with me, or . . . just gentle.

JULIAN *(Softly, a little sadly)*

I don't understand anything. The chapel was in flames.

MISS ALICE

Yes.

JULIAN

. . . and yet . . . I saw the fire here in the model . . . and yet . . . the real chapel was in flames. We put it out. And now the fire here is out as well.

MISS ALICE
(Preceded by a brief, hysterical laugh)

. . . yes.

JULIAN
(Underneath the wonder, some fear)

I don't understand.

MISS ALICE
(She is shivering a little)

It's very hard. Is the chapel saved?

JULIAN
(His attention on the model)

Hm? Oh, yes . . . partially, mostly. The . . . the boards, floorboards, around the altar were . . . gave way, were burned through. The altar . . . sank, some, angled down into the burned-through floor. Marble.

MISS ALICE *(Almost a whisper)*

But the fire is out.

JULIAN

Yes. Out. The spiders, burned to a crisp, I should say, curled-up, burned balls. *(Asking the same question)* I . . . I don't understand.

MISS ALICE
(Vaguely to the model)

It is all well. We are not . . . consumed.

JULIAN

Miss Alice? Why, why did it happen that way—in both dimensions?

MISS ALICE
(Her arms out to him)

Help me.

> *(JULIAN goes to her, lifts her by the arms; they stand, at arm's length, holding hands, facing each other)*

JULIAN

Will you . . . tell me anything?

MISS ALICE
(A helpless laugh, though sad)

I don't know anything.

JULIAN

But you were . . . *(Stops)*

MISS ALICE *(Pleading)*

I don't *know* anything.

JULIAN *(Gently, to placate)*

Very well.

MISS ALICE
(Coming closer to him)

Come stay.

JULIAN

Miss Alice?

MISS ALICE

Come stay here. It will . . . be easier. For you.

JULIAN *(Concern, not anger)*

Did he hurt you?

MISS ALICE

Easier than going back and forth. And for me, too.

JULIAN

Did he?

MISS ALICE
(After a pause and a sad smile)

Some. You're shivering, Julian.

JULIAN

No, Miss Alice, it is *you* . . . you are shivering.

MISS ALICE

The Cardinal will agree to it.

JULIAN
(Looking toward the model)

Yes, I . . . suppose so.

MISS ALICE

Are you frightened, Julian?

JULIAN

Why, no, I . . . I *am* shivering, am I not?

MISS ALICE
Yes.

JULIAN
But I am not . . . yes, I suppose I am . . . frightened.

MISS ALICE
Of what, Julian?

JULIAN
(Looks toward the model again)
But there is . . . *(Back)* . . . of what.

MISS ALICE
Yes.

JULIAN *(Knowing there is)*
Is there anything to be frightened of, Miss Alice?

MISS ALICE *(After a long pause)*
Always.

CURTAIN

Scene Two

(The library—as of Act One, Scene Two. The BUTLER *is on stage. The* LAWYER *enters immediately, angry, impatient)*

LAWYER

Well, where are they today?

BUTLER *(Calm, uninvolved)*

Hm? Who?

LAWYER

WHERE IS SHE! Where is she off to now?

BUTLER

Miss Alice? Well, I don't really know. *(Thinks about it)* You look around?

LAWYER

They're not here.

BUTLER

You don't think they've eloped, do you?

LAWYER

Do you know!

BUTLER

They're moving together nicely; the fire in the chapel helped, I thought, though maybe it was intended to . . . brought them closer.

LAWYER

Where are they!

BUTLER

They spend so much time together now; everything on schedule.

LAWYER

Where have they gone!

BUTLER

I don't *know;* really. Out walking? In the gardens? Driving somewhere? Picnicking, maybe? Cold chicken, cheese, a Montrachet under an elm? I don't *know* where they are.

LAWYER

Don't you watch them?

BUTLER

Keep one eye peeled? Can't she take care of herself? She knows her business. *(Pause; then, quietly meaningful)* Doesn't she. *(No answer)* Doesn't she.

LAWYER

You should watch them. We don't want . . . error. She *is* . . .

BUTLER

Human? Yes, and clever, too . . . isn't she. *Good* at it, wrapping around fingers, enticing. I recall.

LAWYER

Too human; not playing it straight.

BUTLER

Enjoying her work a little? They're not sleeping together yet.

LAWYER

NO! NOT YET!

BUTLER *(A quiet warning)*

Well, it won't bother you when they do . . . will it.

LAWYER *(Matter-of-factly)*

I, too: human.

BUTLER

Human, but dedicated.

LAWYER *(Quiet, sick loathing)*

He doesn't deserve her.

BUTLER *(Kindly)*

Well, he'll not have her long.

LAWYER *(Weary)*

No; not long.

BUTLER

On . . . and on . . . we go.

LAWYER *(Sad)*

Yes.

BUTLER *(Too offhand, maybe)*

I've noticed, you've let your feelings loose lately; too much: possessiveness, jealousy.

LAWYER

I'm *sorry.*

BUTLER

You used to be so good.

LAWYER

I'm SORRY!

BUTLER

It's all right; just watch it.

LAWYER

Attrition: the toll time takes.

BUTLER

I watch you carefully—you, too—and it's the oddest thing: you're a cruel person, straight through; it's not cover; you're hard and cold, saved by dedication; just that.

LAWYER *(Soft sarcasm)*

Thank you.

BUTLER

You're welcome, but what's happened is you're acting like the man you wish you were.

LAWYER

Yes?

BUTLER

Feeling things you can't feel. Why don't you mourn for what you are? There's lament enough there.

LAWYER *(A sad discovery)*

I've never liked you.

BUTLER *(A little sad, too)*

I don't mind. We get along. The three of us.

LAWYER

She's *using* Julian! To humiliate me.

BUTLER *(Nodding)*

Of course. Humiliate; not hurt. Well, let her do her job the way she wants; she'll lead him, bring him around to it.

LAWYER

But she *cares* for him.

BUTLER

Of course; human, a woman. Cares, but it won't get in the way. Let her use what she can. It will be done. Don't you think it's time you went to see His Holiness again?

LAWYER

Eminence, not Holiness. You think it's time I went again?
Yes; well, it *is* time. You come, too.

BUTLER *(Mildly taunting)*

But shouldn't I stay here . . . to watch? To fill you in
on the goings on? To let you be the last to know?

LAWYER

YOU COME! To back me up, when I want emphasis.

BUTLER

In the sense that my father used the word? Wants emphasis: lacks emphasis?

LAWYER

No. The touch of the proletarian: your simplicity, guile-
lessness . . .

BUTLER

Aw . . .

LAWYER

His Eminence is a pompous ass.

BUTLER

Stupid? I doubt *that*.

LAWYER

Not stupid; an ass.

BUTLER

Cardinals aren't stupid; takes brains to get there; no jokes
in the Church.

LAWYER

Pompous!

BUTLER

Well, in front of you, maybe. Maybe has to wear a face;
you're not easy. What will you tell him?

LAWYER
What will I tell him? Tell me.

BUTLER
All right. You play Cardinal, I'll play you.

LAWYER
(Goes into it eagerly; with a laugh)
Ah, two of you. We are doubly honored. Will you not sit?

BUTLER
Really? Like that?

LAWYER
And how is our Brother Julian faring . . . in the world
of the moneyed and the powerful?

BUTLER
No. Really?

LAWYER
Really! And can we be of service to you, further service?

BUTLER
Maybe.

LAWYER
Maybe? Ah?

BUTLER
Yes, your Brother Julian is going to be taken from you.

LAWYER
Our Brother Julian? Taken? From us?

BUTLER
Come on, Your Eminence.

LAWYER
This is a . . . preposterous . . . We . . . we don't
understand you.

BUTLER

Isn't the grant enough? Isn't a hundred million a year for twenty years enough? For one man? He's not even a priest.

LAWYER *(As the CARDINAL)*

A man's soul, Sir! *(Himself)* Not his soul, mustn't say that to him.

BUTLER *(Musing)*

Shall we be dishonest? Well, then, I suppose you'll have to tell him more. Tell him the whole thing.

LAWYER *(Himself)*

I will like that. It will blanch his goddam robes . . . turn 'em white.

BUTLER *(Chuckles)*

Nice when you can enjoy your work, isn't it? Tell him that Julian is leaving him. That Julian has found what he's after. *(Walks to the model, indicates it.)* And I suppose you'd better tell him about . . . this, too.

LAWYER

The wonders of the world?

BUTLER

I think he'd better know . . . about this.

LAWYER

Shatter.

BUTLER

And, you know what I think would be a lovely touch?

LAWYER
(A quiet smile that is also a grimace)

Tell me.

BUTLER

How eager you are. I think it would be a lovely touch
were the Cardinal to marry them, to perform the wedding,
to marry Julian to . . .

LAWYER

Alice.

BUTLER

Miss Alice.

LAWYER

Alice!

BUTLER

Well, all right; one through the other. But have him
marry them.

LAWYER *(Smiles a little)*

It would be nice.

BUTLER

I thought so.

LAWYER

But *shall* we tell him the whole thing? The Cardinal?
What is happening?

BUTLER

How much can he take?

LAWYER

He is a man of God, however much he simplifies, however much he worships the symbol and not the substance.

BUTLER

Like everyone.

LAWYER

Like most.

BUTLER

Julian can't stand that; he told me so: men make God in their own image, he said. Those six years I told you about.

LAWYER

Yes. When he went into an asylum. YES.

BUTLER

It was—because he could not stand it, wasn't it? The use men put God to.

LAWYER

It's perfect; wonderful.

BUTLER

Could not reconcile.

LAWYER

No.

BUTLER

God as older brother, scout leader, couldn't take that.

LAWYER

And still not reconciled.

BUTLER

Has pardoned men, I think. Is walking on the edge of an abyss, but is balancing. Can be pushed . . . over, back to the asylums.

LAWYER

Or over . . . to the Truth *(Addressing* JULIAN, *as if he were there; some thunder in the voice)* God, Julian? Yes? God? *Whose* God? Have you pardoned men their blasphemy, Julian? Have you forgiven them?

BUTLER
(Quiet echoing answers; being JULIAN*)*
No, I have not, have not really; have *let* them, but cannot accept.

LAWYER
Have not forgiven. No, Julian. Could you ever?

BUTLER *(Ibid.)*
It is their comfort; my agony.

LAWYER
Soft God? The servant? Gingerbread God with the raisin eyes?

BUTLER *(Ibid.)*
I cannot accept it.

LAWYER
Then don't accept it, Julian.

BUTLER
But there is *something*. There is a *true* God.

LAWYER
There is an abstraction, Julian, but it cannot be understood. You cannot worship it.

BUTLER *(Ibid.)*
There is more.

LAWYER
There is Alice, Julian. That can be understood. Only the mouse in the model. Just that.

BUTLER *(Ibid.)*
There must be more.

LAWYER

The mouse. Believe it. Don't personify the abstraction, Julian, limit it, demean it. Only the mouse, the toy. And that does not exist . . . but is all that can be worshiped. . . . Cut off from it, Julian, ease yourself, ease off. No trouble now; accept it.

BUTLER
(Talking to JULIAN *now)*
Accept it, Julian; ease off. Worship it . . .

LAWYER

Accept it.

BUTLER
(After a pause; normal again)
Poor, poor Julian.

LAWYER *(Normal, too)*

He can make it.

BUTLER

I hope he can.

LAWYER

If not? *(Shrugs)* Out with him.

BUTLER *(Pause)*
You cannot tell the Cardinal . . . that.

LAWYER *(Weary)*

The benefits to the Church.

BUTLER

Not simply that.

LAWYER
And a man's soul. If it be saved . . . what matter how?

BUTLER
Then we'd best go to him.

LAWYER
Yes.

BUTLER
Leave Julian to Miss Alice; he is in good hands.

LAWYER
(Quiet, sick rage rising)
But his hands . . . on her.

BUTLER *(Soothing)*
Temporary . . . temporal. You'll have her back.

LAWYER *(Rises)*
All right.

BUTLER
Let's go.

LAWYER
*(Walks to the model, addresses it; quietly, but
forcefully; no sarcasm)*
Rest easy; you'll have him . . . Hum; purr; breathe;
rest. You will have your Julian. Wait for him. He will be
yours.

CURTAIN

Scene Three

(MISS ALICE'S *sitting room, as of Act One,
Scene Three.* JULIAN *is on stage, near the fireplace, carries a riding crop; the door to the bedroom is ajar)*

JULIAN
(After a moment; over his shoulder)
It was fun, Miss Alice; it was fun.

MISS ALICE
(From behind the door)
What, Julian?

JULIAN *(Turns)*
It was . . . I enjoyed it; very much.

MISS ALICE
(Her head appearing from behind the door)
Enjoyed what?

JULIAN
Riding; it was . . . exhilarating.

MISS ALICE
I would never have thought you rode. You were good.
(Disappears)

JULIAN
(A small, self-deprecating laugh)
Oh. Yes. When I was young—a child—I knew a family
who . . . kept horses, as a pastime, not as a business.
They were moneyed—well, had *some*. It was one of their
sons who was my playmate . . . and we would ride.

MISS ALICE
(Still behind the door)

Yes.

JULIAN

You remember, you know how seriously children talk, the cabalas we have . . . had. My friends and I would take two hunters, and we would go off for hours, and talk ourselves into quite a state—mutually mesmerizing, almost an hysteria. We would forget the time, and bring the animals back quite lathered. *(Laughs)* We would be scolded—no: cursed *out*—by one groom or another; usually by a great dark Welshman—a young fellow who always scowled and had—I remember it clearly, for I found it remarkable—the hairiest hands I have ever seen, with hair—and this is what I found most remarkable— tufts of coarse black hair on his thumbs. *(Looks at his own thumbs)* Not down, or a few hairs, which many of us have, but tufts. This Welshman.

MISS ALICE
(Head appearing again)

D. H. Lawrence.

JULIAN

Pardon?

MISS ALICE
(Appearing, wearing a black negligee with great sleeves)

"Love on the Farm." Don't you know it?
    (Circles him as she recites it; mock-stalks him)
"I hear his hand on the latch, and rise from my chair
Watching the door open . . .
He flings the rabbit soft on the table board
And comes toward me: he! the uplifted sword
Of his hand against my bosom! . . .

. . . With his hand he turns my face to him
And caresses me with his fingers that still smell grim
Of rabbit's fur! . . .
And down his mouth comes on my mouth! and down
His bright dark eyes over me . . .
. . . his lips meet mine, and a flood
Of sweet fire sweeps across me, so I drown
Against him, die and find death good!"
                        (Cocks her head, smiles)
No?

                    JULIAN *(Embarrassed)*
That was . . . not quite my reaction.

                    MISS ALICE
                (A great, crystal laugh)
No! Silly Julian! No. *(Conspiratorial)* That was a verse I
knew at school, that I memorized. "And down his mouth
comes on my mouth." Oh! That would excite us so . . .
at school; things like that. *(Normal tone; a shrug, a
smile)* Early eroticism; mental sex play.

                    JULIAN *(Still embarrassed)*
Yes.

                    MISS ALICE
I've embarrassed you!

                    JULIAN
No! No!

                    MISS ALICE
Poor Julian; I have. And you were telling me about horseback riding.

                    JULIAN
No, I was telling you about the groom, as far as that goes.
And I suppose . . . yes, I suppose . . . those thumbs

were . . . erotic for *me*—at that time, if you think about it; mental sex play. Unconscious.

MISS ALICE
(Sweetly, to divert him)
It *was* fun riding. *Today.*

JULIAN
Yes!

MISS ALICE
I am fond of hair—man's body hair, except that on the back. *(Very offhand)* Are you hairy, Julian?

JULIAN
I . . . my chest is rather nice, but my arms are . . . surprisingly hairless.

MISS ALICE
And you have no back hair.

JULIAN
Well . . . do you really wish to know?

MISS ALICE *(With a laugh)*
Yes!

JULIAN *(Nods in acquiescence)*
I have no . . . back hair, in the usual sense—of the shoulders . . .
(MISS ALICE nods)
. . . but there is hair, at the small of the back . . . rising.

MISS ALICE
Yes, yes, well, *that* is nice. *(Laughs, points to the crop)* You're carrying the crop. Are you still in the saddle?

JULIAN

(Laughing; shyly brandishing the crop)

Are you one of Mr. Lawrence's ladies? Do you like the
smell of saddle soap, and shall I take my crop to you?

MISS ALICE

(Briefest pause; testing)

Would you?

JULIAN *(Halfhearted laugh)*

MISS ALICE!

MISS ALICE

Nobody does things naturally any more—so few people
have the grace. A man takes a whip to you—a loving
whip, you understand—and you *know,* deep and sadly,
that it's imitation—literary, seen. *(Intentionally too much)*
No one has the natural graces any more.

JULIAN

(Putting the crop down; quietly)

I have . . . not whipped . . .

MISS ALICE

But surely you have.

JULIAN *(An apology)*

I do not recall.

MISS ALICE *(Expansive)*

Oh, my Julian! How many layers! Yes?

JULIAN

We . . . simplify our life . . . as we grow older.

MISS ALICE *(Teasing him)*

But from understanding and acceptance; not from . . .
emptying ourselves.

JULIAN

There are many ways.

MISS ALICE *(Showing her outfit)*

Do you like this?

JULIAN

It is most . . . becoming.

MISS ALICE *(Giggles)*

We're dressed quite alike.

JULIAN *(He, too)*

But the effect is not the same.

MISS ALICE

No. It *is* easier for you living here . . . isn't it?

JULIAN

It's . . . more than a person could want—or *should*
want, which is something we must discuss.

MISS ALICE
(Sensing a coming disappointment)

Oh . . .

JULIAN

Really.

MISS ALICE *(Not pleasantly)*

What do we do wrong?

JULIAN

One of the sins is gluttony . . .

MISS ALICE

Are you getting a belly?

JULIAN
(Smiles, but won't be put off)
. . . and it has many faces—or many bellies, if you wish.
It's a commonplace that we can have too much of things,
and I have too much . . . of comfort, of surroundings,
of ease, of kindness . . . of happiness. I am filled to
bursting.

MISS ALICE *(Hard)*
I think perhaps you misunderstand why you're here.
You're *not* here to . . . to indulge yourself, to . . .

JULIAN *(Tight-lipped)*
I'm aware of that.

MISS ALICE
. . . to . . . to ease in. You're here in service to your
Church.

JULIAN
I've not lost sight of my function.

MISS ALICE
I wonder!

JULIAN *(Really quite angry)*
And *I* wonder! What's being *done* to me. Am I . . . am
I being temp—tested in some fashion?

MISS ALICE *(Jumping on it)*
Tempted?

JULIAN
Tested in some fashion?

MISS ALICE
TEMPTED?

JULIAN

BOTH! Tested! What! My . . . my sincerity, my . . . my other cheek? You have allowed that . . . that *man,* your . . . your lover, to . . . ridicule me. You have per-*mit*ted it.

MISS ALICE

I? Permit?

JULIAN

You have allowed him to abuse me, my position, his, the Church; you have tolerated it, and *smiled.*

MISS ALICE

Tolerate!

JULIAN

And smiled. WHY AM I BEING TESTED! . . . And why am I being tempted? By luxury, by ease, by . . . content . . . by things I do not care to discuss.

MISS ALICE *(Unsympathetic)*

You're answerable to your own temptations.

JULIAN

Yes?

MISS ALICE
(Singsong and patronizing)

Or God is.
(JULIAN snorts)
No? God is not? Is not answerable?

JULIAN

Knows. But is not answerable. I.

MISS ALICE *(Softening some)*

Then *be* answerable.

JULIAN

To my temptations, I am. *(To himself more than to her)*
It would be so easy to . . . fall in, to . . . accept these
surroundings. Oh, life would speed by!

MISS ALICE

With all the ridicule?

JULIAN

That aside.

MISS ALICE

You *have* a friend here . . . as they put it.

JULIAN *(Smiles)*

Butler. Yes; he's nice.

MISS ALICE *(A little laugh)*

I meant me.

JULIAN

Well, of *course.* . . .

MISS ALICE

Or, do you think of me otherwise? Do *I* tempt you?

JULIAN

You, Miss Alice?

MISS ALICE

Or, is it merely the fact of temptation that upsets you so?

JULIAN

I have longed . . . to be of great service. When I was
young—and very prideful—I was filled with a self-im-
portance that was . . . well disguised. Serve. That was
the active word: I would serve! *(Clenches his fist)* I

would serve, and damn anyone or anything that stood
in my way. I would shout my humility from the roof
and break whatever rules impeded my headlong rush
toward obedience. I suspect that had I joined the Trap-
pist order, where silence is the law, I would have chat-
tered about it endlessly. I was impatient with God's
agents, and with God, too, I see it now. A . . . novice
porter, ripping suitcases from patrons' hands, cursing
those who preferred to carry some small parcel for their
own. And I was blind to my pride, and intolerant of any
who did not see me as the humblest of men.

                    MISS ALICE *(A little malice)*
You phrase it so; I suspect you've said it before.

                    JULIAN
Doubtless I have. Articulate men often carry set para-
graphs.

                    MISS ALICE
Pride still.

                    JULIAN
Some.

                    MISS ALICE
And how did your ambition sit?

                    JULIAN
Ambition? Was it?
    (MISS ALICE *displays a knee casually;* JULIAN *jumps)*
What are you doing!

                    MISS ALICE *(Vague flirting)*
I'm . . . sorry.

                    JULIAN
Well. Ambition, yes, I suppose—ambition to be nothing,

to be least. Most obedient, humblest. How did it sit?
For some, patiently, but not well. For me? Even less well.
But I . . . learned.

MISS ALICE

To . . . subside. Is that the simplification you mentioned
before? Of your life. To subside . . . and vanish; to
leave no memory.

JULIAN

No; I wish to leave a . . . memory—of work, of things
done. I've told you; I wish to be of great service, to move
great events; but when it's all time for crediting, I'd like
someone to say no more than "Ah, wasn't there someone
involved in this, who brought it all about? A priest?
Ah-*ha,* a *lay* brother—was that it." *(Smiles)* Like that.
The memory of someone who helped.

MISS ALICE
(Pauses, then laughs)

You're lying!

JULIAN

I?
(Then they both laugh, like conspiratorial children)

MISS ALICE

Every monster was a man first, Julian; every dictator was
a colonel who vowed to retire once the revolution was
done; it's so easy to postpone elections, little brother.

JULIAN

The history of the Church . . .

MISS ALICE

The history of the Church shows half its saints were
martyrs, martyred either for the Church, or by it. The

chronology is jammed with death-seekers and hysterics:
the bloodbath to immortality, Julian. Joan was only one
of the suicides.

JULIAN
(Quivering with intensity)
I WISH TO SERVE AND . . . BE FORGOTTEN.

MISS ALICE
(Comes over, strokes his cheek)
Perhaps you will, Julian.
*(He takes her hand, kisses it, puts it back on
his cheek)*
Yes?

JULIAN *(Guiltily)*
I wish to be of service. *(A little giggle)* I *do.*

MISS ALICE
And be forgotten.

JULIAN
Yes.

MISS ALICE *(Stroking his head)*
Not even remembered a little? By some? As a gentle man,
gentle Julian . . .

JULIAN
Per . . . perhaps.

MISS ALICE
. . . my little lay brother and expert on wines; my
little horseback rider and crop switcher . . .

JULIAN *(As she ruffles his hair)*
Don't . . . do that.

                 MISS ALICE *(Ruffles harder)*
My little whipper, and RAPIST?

                 JULIAN *(Rising, moving away)*
DON'T!

                 MISS ALICE *(Pouting, advancing)*
Julian . . .

                 JULIAN
No, now; no.

                 MISS ALICE *(Still pouting)*
Julian, come kiss me.

                 JULIAN
Please!

                 MISS ALICE *(Singsong)*
Come kiss.

                 JULIAN *(A plea)*
Miss Alice . . . Just . . . let me do my service, and let
me go.

                 MISS ALICE
         (Abruptly to business; not curt, though)
But you're *doing* great service. Not many people have
been put in the position you've been graced by—not
many. Who knows—had some lesser man than you come,
some bishop, all dried and salted, clacketing phrases from
memory, or . . . one of those insinuating super-salesmen
your Church uses, had one of them come . . . who
knows? Perhaps the whole deal would have gone out the
window.

JULIAN

Surely, Miss Alice, you haven't been playing games with
. . . so monumental a matter.

MISS ALICE

The rich are said to be quixotic, the very wealthy cruel,
overbearing; who is to say—might not vast wealth, the
insulation of it, make one quite mad? Games? Oh, no,
my little Julian, there are no games played here; this is
for keeps, and in dead earnest. There *are* cruelties, for
the insulation breeds a strange kind of voyeurism; and
there is impatience, too, over the need to accomplish
what should not be explained; and, at the end of it, a
madness of sorts . . . but a triumph.

JULIAN *(Hands apart)*

Use me, then . . . for the triumph.

MISS ALICE
(Moving on him again)

You are *being* used, my little Julian. *I* am being used . . .
my little Julian. You want to be . . . employed, do you
not? Sacrificed, even?

JULIAN

I have . . . there are no secrets from you, Miss Alice
. . . I have . . . dreamed of sacrifice.

MISS ALICE
(She touches his neck)

Tell me.

JULIAN

You mustn't do . . . it is not wise . . .

MISS ALICE

Tell me.

(She will circle him, touch him occasionally, kiss the back of his neck once during the next speech)

JULIAN

Still my pride . . . a vestige of it.
(He becomes quite by himself during this; unaware of her)
Oh, when I was still a child, and read of the Romans, how they used the saints as playthings—enraged children gutting their teddy bears, dashing the head of their doll against the bedpost, I could . . . I could entrance myself, and see the gladiator on me, his trident fork against my neck, and hear, even hear, as much as feel, the prongs as they entered me; the . . . the beast's saliva dripping from the yellow teeth, the slack sides of the mouth, the . . . sweet, warm breath of the lion; great paws on my spread arms . . . even the rough leather of the pads; and to the point of . . . as the great mouth opened, the breath no longer warm but hot, the fangs on my jaw and forehead, positioned . . . IN. And as the fangs sank in, the great tongue on my cheek and eye, the splitting of the bone, and the *blood* . . . just before the great sound, the coming dark and the silence. I could . . . experience it all. And was . . . engulfed. *(A brief laugh, but not breaking the trance)* Oh, martyrdom. To be that. To be able . . . to be that.

MISS ALICE
(Softly, into his ear; he does not hear it)
Marry me, Julian.

JULIAN

The . . . death of the saints . . . was always the beginning of their lives. To go bloodstained and worthy . . . upward. I could feel the blood on my robes as I went; the smell of the blood, as intense as paint . . . and warm . . . and painless.

MISS ALICE

Marry me.

JULIAN

"Here. I have come. You see my robes? They're red, are they not? Warm? And are not the folds caught together . . . as the blood coagulates? The . . . fingers of my left hand—of both!—are . . . are hard to move apart, as the blood holds finger to finger. And there is a wound in me, the warm dark flow . . . runs down my belly . . . to . . . bathing my groin. You see? I have come . . . bloodstained and worthy."

MISS ALICE

Marry me.

JULIAN *(Still self-tranced)*

Bathed . . . my groin. And as the thumbs of the gladiator pressed . . . against . . . my neck, I . . . as the lion's belly pressed on my chest, I . . . as the . . . I . . . or as the woman sank . . . on the mossy hillock by the roses, and the roar is the crunching growl is the moan is the sweat-breathing is the . . .

MISS ALICE

(Behind him, her arms around his neck, on his chest)

. . . sweat-breathing on the mossy hillock and the white mist in the perfumes . . .

JULIAN

. . . fumes . . . lying . . . on the moss hill in the white filmy gladiator's belly pressing on the chest fanged and the soft hard tongue and the *blood* . . . ENTERS . . . *(Lurches from the chair)* . . . STOP! . . . THAT!

MISS ALICE

(Coming at him slowly)

Come to Alice, Julian, in your sacrifice . . .

JULIAN
(Moving away, but helpless)
Stay . . . away . . . stay.

MISS ALICE
. . . give yourself to her, Julian . . .

JULIAN
. . . a . . . away . . .

MISS ALICE *(Sweetly singsong)*
Come marry Alice, she wants you so; she says she wants
you so, come give yourself to Alice; oh, Alice needs you
and your sacrifice . . .

JULIAN
. . . no . . . no . . .

MISS ALICE
. . . Alice says she wants you, come to Alice, Alice
tells me so, she wants you, come to Alice . . .

JULIAN
. . . no . . . sacrifice . . .

MISS ALICE
Alice tells me so, instructs me, come to her.
*(MISS ALICE has her back to the audience,
JULIAN facing her, but at a distance; she takes
her gown and, spreading her arms slowly, opens
the gown wide; it is the unfurling of great wings)*

JULIAN
(Shaking, staring at her body)
. . . and . . . sacrifice . . . on the altar of . . .

MISS ALICE
Come . . . come . . .

JULIAN

. . . the . . . Lord . . . God . . . in . . . Heaven . . .

MISS ALICE

Come . . .

> (JULIAN *utters a sort of dying cry and moves,*
> *his arms in front of him, to* MISS ALICE; *when*
> *he reaches her, she enfolds him in her great*
> *wings)*

MISS ALICE *(Soothing)*

You will be hers; you will sacrifice yourself to her . . .

JULIAN *(Muffled)*

Oh my God in heaven . . .

MISS ALICE
(Her head going back, calling out)

Alice! . . . Alice? . . .

JULIAN
(Slowly kneeling within the great wings)

. . . in . . . my . . . sacrifice . . .

MISS ALICE *(Still calling out)*

He will be yours! He will be yours! AAALLLIIICCCEEE!

CURTAIN

ACT THREE

(The library, as of Act One, Scene Two. No one on stage. After a moment or so, BUTLER *enters, carrying what looks to be a pile of gray sheets. They are clearly quite heavy. He sets them down on a table, straightens his shoulders from the effort, looks at various chairs, turns to counting the pile.* JULIAN *enters, at more than a casual pace, dressed in a suit)*

JULIAN

Butler!

BUTLER
(Deliberate pause; then)
... four ... five ... six ... *(Pretending suddenly to see* JULIAN*)* Oh! Hello there.

JULIAN

Where ... I ... I feel quite *lost.*

BUTLER *(No comment)*

Why?

JULIAN *(Agitation underneath)*

Well, uh ... I will confess I haven't participated in ... been married before, but ... I can't imagine it's usual for everyone to disap*pear.*

BUTLER

Has everyone?

JULIAN

Yes! *(Quieter)* Yes, I ... per—perhaps His Eminence is occupied, or has *busi*ness—that's it!—has business with

. . . but—but why *she* should . . . There I was . . . one moment married, flooded with white, and . . . then . . . the next, alone. Quite alone, in the . . . echoes.

BUTLER

There is an echo, sometimes, all through it, down every long hall, up in the huge beams . . .

JULIAN

But to be left alone!

BUTLER

Aren't you used to that?

JULIAN

Suddenly!

BUTLER *(Sad smile)*

Like a little boy? When the closet door swings shut after him? Locking him in the dark?

JULIAN

Hm? Yes . . . yes, like that. *(Shudders a little)* Terrifying.

BUTLER

And it's always remote, an attic closet, where one should not have been, where no one can hear, and is not likely to come . . . for a very long time.

JULIAN *(Asking him to stop)*

Yes!

BUTLER
(To the sheets again counting them)

We learn so early . . . are *told,* where not to go, the things we should not do. And there's often a reason.

JULIAN

And *she* vanished as well.

BUTLER

Who?

JULIAN

My . . . my wife.

BUTLER

And who is that?

JULIAN
(As if BUTLER *had forgotten everything)*
Miss Alice!

BUTLER

Ah. Really?

JULIAN

Butler, you saw the wedding!

BUTLER *(Puzzles it a moment)*
Quite so; I did. We. . . Well. Perhaps Miss Alice is changing.

JULIAN

She *must* be; of course. But . . . for everyone to . . . vanish, as if I'd turned my back for a *moment,* and an hour elapsed, or a . . . dimension had . . .

BUTLER *(Passing it over)*
Yes, a dimension—well, that happens.

JULIAN *(Still preoccupied)*
Yes, she must be . . . upstairs. What . . . what are you doing?

BUTLER

What?

JULIAN

What are those?

BUTLER

These? *(Looks at them)* Uh . . . sheets, or covers, more accurately.

JULIAN
(Still quite nervous, staying away)
What are they for?

BUTLER

To . . . cover.

JULIAN *(Ibid.)*

Cover *what!*

BUTLER

Oh . . . nothing; no matter. Housework, that's all. One of my labors.

JULIAN

I . . . I would have thought you'd have champagne . . . ready, that you'd be busy with the party. . . .

BUTLER

One does *many* things. You'll have your champagne, sir, never fear.

JULIAN

I'm sorry; I . . . I was so upset.

BUTLER

Yes.

JULIAN *(Attempting a joke)*

After all, I've not been married before.

BUTLER

No.

JULIAN

And the procedures are a little . . . well, you know.

BUTLER

Yes.

JULIAN

. . . *still* . . .

BUTLER

Yes.

JULIAN

It all *does* seem odd.

BUTLER

Marriage is a confusing business.

JULIAN

Have . . . have you been . . . married?

(BUTLER *gives a noncommittal laugh as answer)*

I . . . I don't know if marriage is, but certainly the circumstances surrounding this *wedding* are rather . . .

BUTLER *(A fairly chilling smile)*

Special people, special problems.

JULIAN *(Hurt)*

Oh. Well . . . yes.

BUTLER *(Disdainful curiosity)*

Do you . . . *feel* married?

JULIAN *(Withdrawn)*

Not having been, I cannot say. *(Pause)* Can I?

BUTLER
*(Takes one of the sheets, opens it with a crack-
ing sound, holds it in front of him, a hand on
each shoulder)*

No. *(Puts it to one side)* I suppose not.

JULIAN

No. I wonder if . . . I wonder if you could go upstairs,
perhaps, and see if Miss Alice . . . my *wife* . . .
is . . .

BUTLER

No. *(Then, rather stern)* I have much too much work to
do. *(Cheerful)* I'll get you some champagne, though.

JULIAN *(Rather removed)*

No, I'll . . . wait for the others, if they haven't all . . .
disappeared.

BUTLER *(Noncommittal)*

To leave you alone with your bride, on your wedding
night? No; not yet.

JULIAN
*(For something to say, as much as anything,
yet hopeful of an answer, or an explanation)*

Miss Alice . . . chose not to invite . . . friends . . .
to the ceremony.

BUTLER *(Chuckle)*

Ah, no. Alice. . . *Miss* Alice does not have friends; ad-
mirers, yes. Worshipers . . . but not buddies.

JULIAN *(Puzzled)*

I asked her why she had not, and she replied . . .

BUTLER *(Improvising)*

. . . it is you, Julian, who are being married . . . ?

JULIAN
(Too self-absorbed to be surprised)
Yes; something like that.

BUTLER
Your wife is . . . something of a recluse.

JULIAN *(Hopeful)*

But so outgoing!

BUTLER
Yes? Well, then; you will indeed have fun. *(Mock instructions)* Uncover the chandeliers in the ballroom! Lay on some footmen! Unplug the fountains! Trim the maze!

JULIAN
(More or less to himself)
She *must* have friends . . . *(Unsure)* must she not?

BUTLER *(Stage whisper)*
I don't know; no one has ever asked her.

JULIAN *(Laughing nervously)*

Oh, indeed!
*(*MISS ALICE *comes hurriedly into the room; she has on a suit. She sees only* BUTLER *first)*

MISS ALICE
Butler! Have you seen . . . ? *(Sees* JULIAN*)* Oh, I'm . . . sorry. *(She begins to leave)*

JULIAN
There you are. No, wait; wait!

(But MISS ALICE *has left the room. In need of help)*

I find everything today puzzling.

BUTLER *(About to give advice)*

Look . . . *(Thinks better of it)*

JULIAN

Yes?

BUTLER *(Shrugs)*

Nothing. The wages of a wedding day.

JULIAN

Are you my friend?

BUTLER
(Takes a while to think about the answer)

I *am;* yes; but you'll probably think not.

JULIAN

Is something being kept from me?

BUTLER *(After a pause)*

You loathe sham, do you not?

JULIAN

Yes.

BUTLER

As do we all . . . most of us. You are dedicated to the reality of things, rather than their appearance, are you not?

JULIAN

Deeply.

BUTLER

As are . . . some of us.

JULIAN

It was why I retreated . . . withdrew . . . to the asylum.

BUTLER

Yes, yes. And you are devout.

JULIAN

You know that.

BUTLER

When you're locked in the attic, Julian, in the attic closet, in the dark, do you care who comes?

JULIAN

No. But . . .

BUTLER *(Starts to leave)*

Let me get the champagne.

JULIAN

Please!

BUTLER

So that we all can toast.
          (As BUTLER *leaves, the* CARDINAL *enters)*
Ah! Here comes the Church.

JULIAN

(Going to the CARDINAL, *kneeling before him, kissing his ring, holding the ring hand afterward, staying kneeling)*
Your Eminence.

CARDINAL

Julian. Our dear Julian.

BUTLER

Have you caught the bride?

CARDINAL

No. No. Not seen her since the . . . since we married
her.

JULIAN

It was good of you. I suspect she will be here soon.
Butler, would you . . . go see? If she will come here?
His Eminence would . . . Now do be good and go.

(BUTLER exits)

He has been a great help. At times when my service has
. . . perplexed me, till I grew despondent, and wondered
if perhaps you'd not been mistaken in putting such a
burden . . .

CARDINAL
(Not wanting to get into it)

Yes, yes, Julian. We have *resolved* it.

JULIAN

But then I judge it is God's doing, this . . . wrenching
of my life from one light to another . . .

CARDINAL

. . . Julian . . .

JULIAN

. . . though not losing God's light, joining it with . . .
my new. *(He is like a bubbling little boy)* I can't tell you,
the . . . radiance, humming, and the witchcraft, I think
it must be, the ecstasy of this light, as *God's* exactly; the

transport the same, the lifting, the . . . the sense of service, and the EXPANSION . . .

CARDINAL

. . . Julian . . .

JULIAN

. . . the blessed wonder of service with a renewing, not an ending joy—that joy I thought possible only through martyrdom, now, now the sunlight is no longer the hope for glare and choking in the dust and plummeting, but with cool and green and yellow dappled . . . perfumes . . .

CARDINAL *(Sharply)*

Julian!

JULIAN *(Little-boy smile)*

Sir.

CARDINAL
(Evading JULIAN'S *eyes)*

We sign the papers today, Julian. It's all arranged, the grant is accomplished; through your marriage . . . your service.

JULIAN *(Puzzlement)*

Father?

CARDINAL
(Barely keeping pleasure in his voice)

And isn't it wonderful: that you have . . . found yourself such great service and such . . . exceeding happiness, too; that God's way has brought such gifts to his servant, and to his servant's servant as well.

JULIAN *(Puzzled)*

Thank you . . . Your Eminence.

CARDINAL *(Sadly)*

It is your wedding day, Julian!

JULIAN
(Smiles, throws off his mood)

Yes, it is! It's my wedding day. And a day of glory to
God, that His Church has been blessed with great wealth,
for the suffering of the world, conversion and the pro-
nouncement of His Glory.

CARDINAL
(Embarrassed; perfunctory)

Praise God.

JULIAN

That God has seen fit to let me be His instrument in this
undertaking, that God . . .

CARDINAL

Julian. *(Pause)* As you have accepted what has happened
. . . removed, so far removed from . . . any thought
. . . accept what . . . *will* happen, *may* happen, with
the same humility and . . .

JULIAN *(Happily)*

It is my service.

CARDINAL *(Nods)*

Accept what may come . . . as God's will.

JULIAN

Don't . . . don't frighten me. Bless me, Father.

CARDINAL *(Embarrassed)*

Julian, please . . .

JULIAN
(On his knees before the CARDINAL)

Bless me?

CARDINAL
(Reluctantly; appropriate gestures)
In the name of the Father and of the Son and the Holy
Ghost . . .

JULIAN
. . . Amen . . .

CARDINAL
. . . Amen. You *have* . . . confessed, Julian?

JULIAN
(Blushing, but childishly pleased)
I . . . I have, Father; I have . . . confessed, and
finally, to sins more real than imagined, but . . . but
they are not sins, are they, in God's name, done in
God's name, Father?

CARDINAL
May the presence of our Lord, Jesus Christ be with you
always. . .

JULIAN
. . . to . . . to shield my eyes from too much light,
that I may be always worthy . . .

CARDINAL
. . . to light your way for you in the darkness . . .

JULIAN
. . . dark, darkness, Father? . . .

CARDINAL
. . . that you may be worthy of whatever sacrifice, unto
death itself . . .

JULIAN
. . . in all this light! . . .

CARDINAL

. . . is asked of you; that you may accept what you do
not understand . . .

JULIAN *(A mild argument)*

But, Father . . .

CARDINAL

. . . and that the Lord may have mercy on your soul
. . . as, indeed, may He have on us all . . . all our
souls.

JULIAN

. . . A . . . Amen?

CARDINAL *(Nodding)*

Amen.

LAWYER *(Entering)*

Well, well. Your Eminence. Julian. Well, you are indeed
a fortunate man, today. What more cheering sight can
there be than Frank Fearnought, clean-living, healthy
farm lad, come from the heartland of the country, from
the asylums—you see, I know—in search of fame, and
true love—never fortune, of course.

JULIAN

. . . Please . . .

LAWYER

And see what has happened to brave and handsome
Frank: he has found what he sought . . . true . . .
love; *and* fortune—to his surprise, for wealth had never
crossed his pure mind; and fame? . . . Oooooh, there
will be a private fame, perhaps.

CARDINAL

Very pretty.

LAWYER

And we are dressed in city ways, too, are we not? No
longer the simple gown of the farm lad, the hems trailing
in the dung; no; now we are in city clothes . . . banker's
clothes.

JULIAN

These are proper clothes.

LAWYER

As you will discover, poor priestlet, poor former priestlet.
Dressed differently for the sacrifice, eh?

JULIAN

I . . . think I'll . . . look for Miss . . . for my wife.

LAWYER

Do.

CARDINAL

Oh, yes, Julian; please.

JULIAN
(Kneels, kisses the ring again)
Your Eminence. *(To the* LAWYER, *mildly)* We are both
far too old . . . are we not . . . for all that?
(JULIAN exits)

CARDINAL *(After JULIAN leaves)*
Is cruelty a lesson you learned at your mother's knee?
One of the songs you were taught?

LAWYER

One learns by growing, as they say. I have fine instructors
behind me . . . yourself amongst them. *(A dismissing
gesture)* We have no time. *(Raises his briefcase, then
throws it on a table)* All here. *(Great cheerfulness)* All

here! The grant: all your money. *(Normal tone again)* I must say, your Church lawyers are picky men.

CARDINAL

Thorough.

LAWYER

Picky. Humorless on small matters, great wits on the major ones; ribald over the whole proposition.

CARDINAL *(Mumbling)*

. . . hardly a subject for ribaldry . . .

LAWYER

Oh, quite a dowry, greatest marriage settlement in history, *mother* church indeed . . . things like that.

CARDINAL *(Unhappily)*

Well, it's all over now . . .

LAWYER

Almost.

CARDINAL

Yes.

LAWYER

Cheer up; the price was high enough.

CARDINAL

Then it is . . . really true? About . . . *this?* *(Points at the model)*

LAWYER

I haven't time to lie to you.

CARDINAL

Really . . . true.

LAWYER
(Moving to the model)
Really. Can't you accept the wonders of the world? Why not of this one, as well as the other?

CARDINAL
We should be . . . getting on.

LAWYER
Yes. *(Points to a place in the model)* Since the wedding was . . . here . . . and we are *(Indicates the room they are in) here* . . . we have come quite a . . . dimension, have we not?
(The LAWYER *moves away from the model to a table, as the* CARDINAL *stays at the model)*

CARDINAL *(Abstracted)*
Yes. A distance.
(Turns, sees the LAWYER *open a drawer, take out a pistol and check its cartridges)*
What . . . what are you doing? *(Moves toward the* LAWYER, *slowly)*

LAWYER
House pistol.

CARDINAL
But what are you doing?

LAWYER
(Looking it over carefully)
I've never shot one of these things . . . pistols. *(Then, to answer)* I'm looking at it . . . to be sure the cartridges are there, to see that it is oiled, or whatever is done to it . . . to see how it functions.

CARDINAL
But . . .

LAWYER *(Calmly)*

You know we may have to shoot him; you know that
may be necessary.

CARDINAL *(Sadly and softly)*

Dear God, no.

LAWYER *(Looking at the gun)*

I suppose all you do is . . . pull. *(Looks at the CAR-
DINAL)* If the great machinery threatens . . . to come
to a halt . . . the great axis on which all turns . . . if
it needs oil . . . well, we lubricate it, do we not? And
if blood is the only oil handy . . . what is a little blood?

CARDINAL *(False bravura)*

But that will not be necessary. *(Great empty quiet loss)*
Dear God, let that not be necessary.

LAWYER

Better off dead, perhaps. You know? Eh?

CARDINAL

The making of a martyr? A saint?

LAWYER

Well, let's make that saint when we come to him.

CARDINAL

Dear God, let that not be necessary.

LAWYER

Why not? Give me *any* person . . . a martyr, if you wish
. . . a saint . . . He'll take what he gets for . . . what
he wishes it to be. AH, it is what I have always wanted,
he'll say, looking terror and betrayal straight in the eye.
Why not: face the inevitable and call it what you have
always wanted. How to come out on top, going under.

(JULIAN enters)

LAWYER

Ah! There you are. Still not with Miss Alice!

JULIAN

I seem not to be with anyone.

LAWYER *(Smile)*

Isn't that odd?

JULIAN
(Turning away, more to himself)

I would have thought it so.

CARDINAL
(Hearty, but ill at ease)

One would have thought to have it all now—corks popping, glasses splintering in the fireplace . . .

LAWYER

When Christ told Peter—so legends tell—that he would found his church upon that rock, He must have had in mind an island in a sea of wine. How firm a foundation in the vintage years . . .
(We hear voices from without; they do, too)

MISS ALICE *(Offstage)*

I don't *want* to go in there . . .

BUTLER *(Offstage)*

You *have* to come in, now . . .

MISS ALICE *(Offstage)*

I won't go *in* there. . . .

BUTLER *(Offstage)*

Come along now; don't be a child. . . .

MISS ALICE *(Offstage)*

I . . . won't . . . *go* . . .
(BUTLER *appears; two champagne bottles in
one hand, pulling* MISS ALICE *with the other)*

BUTLER

Come along!

MISS ALICE
(As she enters; sotto voce)

I don't want to . . .
*(As she sees the others see her, she stops talk-
ing, smiles, tries to save the entrance)*

BUTLER

Lurking in the gallery, talking to the ancestral wall, but
I found her.

MISS ALICE

Don't be silly; I was . . . *(Shrugs)*

BUTLER *(Shrugs, too)*

Suit yourself. Champagne, everybody!

JULIAN

Ah! Good. *(Moving toward* MISS ALICE*)* Are you all
right?

MISS ALICE
(Moves away from him; rather impatiently)

Yes.

CARDINAL

But you've changed your clothes, and your wedding gown
was . . .

MISS ALICE

. . . two hundred years old . . .

LAWYER

. . . fragile.

CARDINAL

Ah!

(Something of a silence falls. The other characters are away from JULIAN; *unless otherwise specified, they will keep a distance, surrounding him, but more than at arm's length. They will observe him, rather clinically, and while this shift of attitude must be subtle, it must also be evident.* JULIAN *will grow to knowledge of it, will aid us, though we will be aware of it before he is)*

JULIAN *(To break the silence)*

Well, shall we have the champagne?

BUTLER

Stay there! *(Pause)* I'll bring it.

CARDINAL

Once, when we were in France, we toured the champagne country . . .

LAWYER *(No interest)*

Really.

CARDINAL

Saw the . . . mechanics, so to speak, of how it was done. . . .

LAWYER

Peasants? Treading?

CARDINAL *(Laughs)*

No, no. That is for woodcuts.

(The cork pops)

Ah!

BUTLER

Nobody move! I'll bring it to you all.
(*Starts pouring into glasses already placed to
the side*)

MISS ALICE (*To the* LAWYER)

The ceremony.
                    (*He does not reply*)
The ceremony!

LAWYER (*Overly sweet smile*)

Yes. (*To them all*) The ceremony.

CARDINAL

Another? Must we officiate?

LAWYER

No need.

JULIAN (*A little apprehensive*)

What . . . ceremony is this?

BUTLER (*His back to them*)

There's never as much in a champagne bottle as I expect
there to be; I never learn. Or, perhaps the glasses are
larger than they seem.

LAWYER (*Ironic*)

When the lights go on all over the world . . . the true
world. The ceremony of Alice.

JULIAN (*To* MISS ALICE)

What is this about?
                    (*She nods toward the* LAWYER)

LAWYER

Butler? Are you poured?

BUTLER
(Finishing; squeezing the bottle)

Yeeeeesssss . . .

LAWYER

Pass.

BUTLER
(Starts passing the tray of glasses)

Miss Alice.

MISS ALICE *(Strained)*

Thank you.

BUTLER
(Starts toward JULIAN, *changes his mind, goes to the* CARDINAL)

Your Eminence?

CARDINAL

Ahhh.

BUTLER
(Starts toward JULIAN *again, changes his mind goes to the* LAWYER)

Sweetheart?

LAWYER

Thank you.

BUTLER
(Finally goes to JULIAN, *holds the tray at arm's length; speaks, not unkindly)*

Our Brother Julian.

JULIAN *(Shy friendliness)*

Thank you, Butler.

LAWYER

And now . . .

BUTLER
(Moving back to the table with the tray)
Hold on; I haven't got mine yet. It's over here.

JULIAN

Yes! Butler must drink with us. *(To* MISS ALICE*)* Don't
you think so?

MISS ALICE *(Curiously weary)*
Why not? He's family.

LAWYER
(Moving toward the model)
Yes; what a large family you have.
   (The LAWYER *would naturally have to pass near*
   JULIAN; *pauses, detours)*

JULIAN

I'm sorry; am . . . am I in your way?

LAWYER
(Continues to the model)
Large family, years of adding. The ceremony, children.
The ceremony of Alice.
   (The others have turned, are facing the model.
   The LAWYER *raises his glass)*
To Julian and his bride.

CARDINAL

Hear, hear.

JULIAN *(Blushing)*
Oh, my goodness.

LAWYER

To Julian and his bride; to Alice's wisdom, wealth and whatever.

BUTLER *(Quietly, seriously)*

To Alice.

MISS ALICE

To Alice.
> *(Brief pause; only* JULIAN *turns his head, is about to speak, but)*

LAWYER

To their marriage. To their binding together, acceptance and worship . . . received; accepted.

BUTLER

To Alice.

LAWYER

To the marriage vow between them, which has brought joy to them both, and great benefit to the Church.

CARDINAL

Amen.

MISS ALICE

To Alice.
> *(Again only* JULIAN *responds to this; a half turn of the head)*

LAWYER

To their house.

BUTLER, MISS ALICE and CARDINAL
> *(Not quite together)*

To their house.

JULIAN *(After them)*

To their house.

LAWYER

To the chapel wherein they were bound in wedlock.
(A light goes on in a room in the model.
JULIAN *makes sounds of amazement; the others*
are silent)
To their quarters.
         (Light goes on upstairs in the model)
To the private rooms where marriage lives.

BUTLER

To Alice.

MISS ALICE

To Alice.
         (To which JULIAN *does not respond this time)*

LAWYER

And to this room . . .
         (Another light goes on in the model)
in which they are met, in which we are met . . . to cele-
brate their coming together.

BUTLER

Amen.

LAWYER

A union whose spiritual values shall be uppermost . . .

MISS ALICE

That's enough . . .

LAWYER

. . . whose carnal side shall . . .

MISS ALICE

That's enough!

JULIAN

May . . . May I?
*(It is important that he stay facing the model,
not* MISS ALICE. BUTLER, *who is behind him,
may look at him; the* CARDINAL *will look to the
floor)*
May I . . . propose. To the wonders . . . which may
befall a man . . . least where he is looking, least that he
would have thought; to the clear plan of that which we
call chance, to what we see as accident till our humility
returns to us when we are faced with the mysteries. To
all that which we really want, until our guile and
pride . . .

CARDINAL
(Still looking at the floor)
. . . Julian . . .

JULIAN

. . . betray us? *(Looks at the* CARDINAL; *pauses, goes on,
smiling sweetly)* My gratitude . . . my wonder . . . and
my love.

LAWYER *(Pause)*

Amen?

JULIAN

Amen.

LAWYER *(Abruptly turning)*
Then, if we're packed, let us go.

BUTLER *(Not moving)*
Dust covers.

JULIAN *(Still smiling)*

Go?

CARDINAL *(To delay)*

Well. *This* champagne glass seems smaller than one would have guessed; it has emptied itself . . . on one toast!

LAWYER

I recall. Suddenly I recall it. When we were children. *(Quite fascinated with what he is saying)* When we were children and we would gather in the dark, two of us . . . any two . . . on a swing, side porch, or by the ocean, sitting backed against a boulder, and we would explore . . . those most private parts, of one another, any two of us . . . *(Shrugs)* boy, girl, how—when we did it—we would talk of other things . . . of our schoolwork, or where we would travel in the summer. How, as our shaking hands passed under skirts or undid buttons, sliding, how we would, both of us, talk of other things, whispering, our voices shaking as our just barely moving hands. *(Laughs, points to the* CARDINAL*)* Like you! Chattering there on the model! Your mind on us and what is happening. Oh, the subterfuges.

MISS ALICE

I am packed.

JULIAN *(Still off by himself)*

Packed? . . . Miss Alice? . .

MISS ALICE
(To the LAWYER; *cold)*

May we leave soon?

JULIAN

Miss . . . Alice?

MISS ALICE

May we?

LAWYER *(Pause)*

Fairly.

JULIAN *(Sharp)*

Miss Alice!

MISS ALICE
(Turns toward him; flat tone; a recitation)
I'm very happy for you, Julian, you've done well.

JULIAN
(Backing away from everyone a little)
What is . . . going on . . . here? *(To* MISS ALICE*)* Tell me!

MISS ALICE
(As if she is not interested)
I am packed. We are going.

JULIAN *(Sudden understanding)*
Ah! *(Points to himself) We* are going. But where? You
. . . didn't tell me we . . . we were . . .

MISS ALICE
(To the LAWYER, *moving away)*
Tell him.

JULIAN

. . . going somewhere. . . .

MISS ALICE *(Quite furious)*

Tell him!

LAWYER
(About to make a speech)
Brother Julian . . .

JULIAN *(Strained)*

I am no longer Brother.

LAWYER *(Oily)*

Oh, are we not all brothers?

JULIAN
(To MISS ALICE; *with a halfhearted gesture)*
Come stand by me.

MISS ALICE
(Surprisingly little-girl fright)

No!

LAWYER

Now. Julian.

CARDINAL

Order yourself, Julian.

JULIAN *(To the* CARDINAL*)*

Sir?

LAWYER
(Sarcasm is gone; all is gone, save fact)
Dear Julian; we all serve, do we not? Each of us his own
priesthood; publicly, some, others . . . within only; but we
all do—what's-his-name's special trumpet, or clear lonely
bell. Predestination, fate, the will of God, accident . . .
All swirled up in it, no matter what the name. And being
man, we have invented choice, and have, indeed, gone further, and have catalogued the underpinnings of choice.
But we do not know. Anything. End prologue.

MISS ALICE

Tell him.

LAWYER

No matter. We are leaving you now, Julian; agents, every
one of us—going. We are leaving you . . . to your

accomplishment: your marriage, your wife, your . . .
special priesthood.

JULIAN
(Apprehension and great suspicion)
I . . . don't know what you're talking about.

LAWYER *(Unperturbed)*
What is so amazing is the . . . coming together . . . of
disparates . . . left-fielding, out of the most unlikely. Who
would have thought, Julian? Who would have thought?
You have brought us to the end of our service here. We
go on; you stay.

BUTLER
May I begin to cover?

MISS ALICE
Not yet. *(Kindly)* Do you understand, Julian?

JULIAN *(Barely in control)*
Of course not!

MISS ALICE
Julian, I have tried to be . . . *her.* No; I have tried to be
. . . what I thought she might, what might make you
happy, what you might use, as a . . . what?

BUTLER
Play God; go on.

MISS ALICE
We must . . . represent, draw pictures, reduce or enlarge
to . . . to what we can understand.

JULIAN *(Sad, mild)*
But I have fought against it . . . all my life. When they
said, "Bring the wonders down to me, closer; I cannot see

them, touch; nor can I believe." I have fought against it
. . . all my life.

BUTLER *(To* MISS ALICE; *softly)*
You see? No good.

MISS ALICE *(Shrugs)*
I have done what I can with it.

JULIAN
All my life. In and out of . . . confinement, fought against
the symbol.

MISS ALICE
Then you should be happy now.

CARDINAL
Julian, it has been your desire always to serve; your sense
of mission . . .

LAWYER
We are surrogates; *our* task is done now.

MISS ALICE
Stay with her.

JULIAN
(Horror behind it; disbelieving)
Stay . . . with . . .her?

MISS ALICE
Stay with her. Accept it.

LAWYER *(At the model)*
Her rooms are lighted. It is warm, there is enough.

MISS ALICE
Be content with it. Stay with her.

JULIAN
(Refusing to accept what he is hearing)
Miss Alice . . . I have married you.

MISS ALICE *(Kind, still)*
No, Julian; you have married *her* . . . through me.

JULIAN
(Pointing to the model)
There is nothing there! We are *here!* There is no one
there!

LAWYER
She is there . . . we believe.

JULIAN *(To* MISS ALICE*)*
I have *been* with *you!*

MISS ALICE
(Not explaining; sort of dreamy)
You have felt her warmth through me, touched her lips
through my lips, held hands, through mine, my breasts,
hers, lain on her bed, through mine, wrapped yourself in
her wings, your hands on the small of her back, your
mouth on her hair, the voice in your ear, hers not mine,
all hers; her. You are hers.

CARDINAL
Accept.

BUTLER
Accept.

LAWYER
Accept.

JULIAN
THERE IS NO ONE THERE!

MISS ALICE

She is there.

JULIAN
(Rushes to the model, shouts at it)
THERE IS NOTHING THERE! *(Turns to them all)* THERE IS
NOTHING THERE!

CARDINAL *(Softly)*

Accept it, Julian

JULIAN *(All the power he has)*

ACCEPT IT!

LAWYER *(Quietly)*
All legal, all accomplished, all satisfied, that which we
believe.

JULIAN

ACCEPT!

BUTLER
. . . that which is done, and may not be revoked.

CARDINAL *(With some difficulty)*
. . . yes.

JULIAN

WHAT AM I TO ACCEPT!

LAWYER

An act of faith.

JULIAN *(Slow, incredulous)*
An . . . act . . . of . . . faith!

LAWYER
(Snaps his fingers at the CARDINAL*)*

Buddy?

CARDINAL

Uh . . . yes, Julian, an . . . act of faith, indeed. It is
. . . believed.

LAWYER
(Deadly serious, but with a small smile)
Yes, it is . . . believed. It is what we believe, therefore
what we know. Is that not right? Faith is knowledge?

CARDINAL

An act of faith, Julian, however we must . . .

JULIAN *(Horror)*

FAITH!?

CARDINAL

. . . in God's will . . .

JULIAN

GOD'S! WILL!

CARDINAL
(As if his ears are hurting, sort of mumbling)
Yes, Julian, you see, we must accept, and . . . be glad,
yes, be glad . . . our ecstasy.

JULIAN
(Backing off a little, shaking his head)
I have not come this distance . . .

CARDINAL
(Moving toward him a little)
Julian . . .

JULIAN

Stay back! I have not come this long way . . . have not—
in all sweet obedience—walked in these . . . *(Realizes he
is differently dressed)* those robes . . . to be MOCKED.

LAWYER

Accept it, Julian.

JULIAN

I have not come this long *way!*

BUTLER

Yes; oh, yes.

JULIAN

I HAVE NOT!

MISS ALICE *(Kindly)*

Julian . . . dear Julian; accept.

JULIAN
(Turns toward her, supplicating)

I have not worn and given up for . . . for mockery; I
have not stretched out the path of my life before me, to
walk on straight, to be . . .

MISS ALICE

Accept.

JULIAN

I have not fought the nightmares—and the waking demons, yes—and the years of despair, those, too . . . I
have not accepted *half,* for *nothing.*

CARDINAL

For everything.

MISS ALICE

Dear Julian; accept. Allow us all to rest.

JULIAN
(A child's terror of being alone)

NO!

MISS ALICE *(Still kind)*

You must.

BUTLER

No choice.

JULIAN

I have . . . have . . . given up everything to gain everything, for the sake of my faith and my peace; I have allowed and followed, and sworn and cherished, but I have
not, have *not* . . .

MISS ALICE

Be with her. Please.

JULIAN

For halluci*nation?* I HAVE DONE WITH HALLUCINATION.

MISS ALICE

Then have done with forgery, Julian; accept what's real.
I am the . . . illusion.

JULIAN *(Retreating)*

No . . . no no no, oh no.

LAWYER *(Quietly)*

All legal, all accomplished, all satisfied, that which we believe.

MISS ALICE

All done.

JULIAN *(Quite frightened)*

I . . . choose . . . *not.*

CARDINAL

There is no choice here, Julian. . . .

LAWYER

No choice at all.

MISS ALICE *(Hands apart)*

All done.

> (JULIAN *begins backing toward the model; the*
> LAWYER *begins crossing to the desk wherein he*
> *has put the gun)*

BUTLER *(Quietly)*

I *must* cover now; the cars are waiting.

JULIAN

No ... no ... I WILL NOT ACCEPT THIS.

LAWYER
(Snaps for the CARDINAL *again)*

Buddy ...

CARDINAL

We ...(*Harder tone*) I *order* you.

LAWYER *(Smile)*

There. Now will you accept?

JULIAN

I . . . cannot be so mistaken, to have . . . I cannot have
so misunderstood my life; I cannot have . . . was I sane
then? Those *years?* My time in the *asylum?* WAS THAT
WHEN I WAS RATIONAL? THEN?

CARDINAL

Julian . . .

LAWYER
(Taking the gun from the drawer, checking it;
to the CARDINAL)

Don't you teach your people anything? Do you let them
improvise? *Make* their Gods? *Make* them as they *see*
them?

JULIAN *(Rage in the terror)*
I HAVE ACCEPTED GOD.

LAWYER
(Turns to JULIAN, *gun in hand)*
Then accept his works. Resign yourself to the myster-
ies . . .

MISS ALICE
. . . to greater wisdom.

LAWYER
Take it! Accept what you're given.

MISS ALICE
Your priesthood, Julian—full, at last. Stay with her. Accept your service.

JULIAN
I . . . cannot . . . accept . . . this.

LAWYER *(Aims)*
Very well, then.

JULIAN
I have not come this . . . given up so much for . . .

BUTLER
Accept it, Julian.

MISS ALICE
Stay with her.

JULIAN
No, no, I will . . . I will go *back!* I will . . . go *back* to

it. (*Starts backing toward the stairs*) To . . . to . . . I will
go back to the asylum.

LAWYER

Last chance.

MISS ALICE

Accept it, Julian.

JULIAN

To . . . my asylum. MY! ASYLUM! My . . . my refuge . . .
in the world, from all the demons waking, my . . .
REFUGE!

LAWYER

Very well then.
> (*Shoots. Then silence.* JULIAN *does not cry out,
> but clutches his belly, stumbles forward a few
> steps, sinks to the floor in front of the model*)

MISS ALICE
> (*Softly, with compassion*)

Oh, Julian. (*To the* LAWYER; *calm*) He would have
stayed.

LAWYER
> (*To* MISS ALICE, *shrugging*)

It was an accident.

JULIAN

Fa . . . ther?

MISS ALICE

Poor Julian. (*To the* LAWYER) You did not have to do
that; I could have made him stay.

LAWYER

Perhaps. But what does it matter . . . one man . . . in
the face of so much.

JULIAN

Fa . . . ther?

BUTLER *(Going to* JULIAN)

Let me look.

MISS ALICE
(Starting to go to him)

Oh, poor JULIAN . . .

LAWYER *(Stopping her)*

Stay where you are.

(BUTLER *goes to* JULIAN *while the others keep
their places.* BUTLER *bends over him, maybe
pulling his head back)*

BUTLER

Do you want a doctor for him?

LAWYER *(After a tiny pause)*

Why?

BUTLER *(Straightening up)*

Because . . .

LAWYER

Yes?

BUTLER *(Quite matter-of-fact)*

Because he will bleed to death without attention?

JULIAN *(To the* CARDINAL)

Help . . . me?

(In answer, the CARDINAL *looks back to the*
LAWYER, *asking a question with his silence)*

LAWYER *(After a pause)*

No doctor.

BUTLER *(Moving away)*

No doctor.

MISS ALICE
(To the LAWYER; *great sadness)*

No?

LAWYER *(Some compassion)*

No.

JULIAN

Father!

CARDINAL *(Anguished)*

Please, Julian.

JULIAN
(Anger through the pain)
In the sight of God? You dare?

LAWYER

Or in the sight of man. He dares. *(Moves to the table, putting the gun away, taking up the briefcase)*

JULIAN *(Again)*

You dare!?
*(*BUTLER *goes to cover something)*

LAWYER
(Taking the briefcase to the CARDINAL*)*
There it is, all of it. All legal now, the total grant: two billion, kid, twenty years of grace for no work at all; no labor . . . at least not yours. *(Holds the briefcase out)* There . . . take it.

CARDINAL

We do not . . . fetch and carry. And have not acquiesced . . . *(Indicates briefcase)* For *this.*

JULIAN *(Weak again)*

Father?

LAWYER

Not God's errand boy?

CARDINAL

God's; not yours.

LAWYER

Who are the Gods?

JULIAN *(Pain)*

God in heaven!

MISS ALICE

Poor Julian!
> *(Goes to him; they create something of a Pietà)*
Rest back; lean on me.

LAWYER
> *(Withdrawing his offer of the briefcase)*
Perhaps your *new* secretary can pick it up. You *will* go
on, won't you—red gown and amethyst, until the pelvic
cancer comes, or the coronary blacks it out, all of it? The
good with it, and the evil? *(Indicates* JULIAN*)* Even this?
In the final mercy?
> *(The* CARDINAL *looks straight ahead of him for
> a moment, hesitates, then walks out, looking
> neither left nor right)*

BUTLER
> *(Calling after him, halfhearted and intentionally
> too late)*
Any of the cars will do . . . *(Trailing off)* . . . as
they're all hired.

JULIAN

Who . . . who left? Who!

MISS ALICE *(Comforting him)*

You're shivering, Julian . . . so.

JULIAN *(Almost a laugh)*

Am I?

LAWYER
(Still looking after the departed CARDINAL*)*

Once, when I was at school—our departed reminds me
—once, when I was at school, I was writing poetry—
well, no, poems, which were published in the literary
magazine. And each issue a teacher from the English
Department would criticize the work in the school news-
paper a week or two hence.

MISS ALICE *(To* JULIAN*)*

A blanket?

JULIAN

No. Hold close.

LAWYER

And one teacher, who was a wag and was, as well, a
former student, wrote of one of my poems—a sonnet, as
I recall—that it had all the grace of a walking crow.

MISS ALICE *(Ibid.)*

I don't want to hurt.

JULIAN

Closer . . . please. Warmth.

LAWYER

I was green in those years, and, besides, I could not recall
how crows walked.

MISS ALICE *(Ibid.)*

How like a little boy you are.

JULIAN

I'm lonely.

LAWYER

Could not recall that I had ever *seen* a crow . . . walking.

MISS ALICE

Is being afraid always the same—no matter the circumstances, the age?

JULIAN

It is the attic room, always; the closet. Hold close.

LAWYER
(Fully aware of the counterpoint by now, aiding it)
And so I went to see him—the wag—about the walking crow . . . the poem, actually.

BUTLER
(Putting a cover on something)
Crows don't walk much . . .

JULIAN

. . . and it is very dark; always. And no one will come . . . for the longest time.

MISS ALICE

Yes.

LAWYER

Yes; that is what he said—sitting with his back against all the books, "Crows don't walk much . . . if they can help it . . . if they can fly."

JULIAN

No. No one will come.

BUTLER (*Snapping open a cover*)
I could have told you that; surprised you didn't know it.
Crows walk around a lot only when they're sick.

LAWYER
"Santayanian finesse."

JULIAN
No one will come . . . for the longest time; if ever.

MISS ALICE (*Agreeing*)
No.

LAWYER
That was the particular thing: "Santayanian finesse." He
said that had . . . all the grace of a walking crow.

BUTLER
(*Rubbing something for dust*)
Bright man.

LAWYER (*To* BUTLER)
I don't know; he stayed on some years after I left—after
our walking bird and I left—then went on to some other
school. . . . (*To* MISS ALICE, *immediately*) Are you
ready to go?

MISS ALICE
(*Looking up; sad irony*)
Am I ready to go on with it, do you mean? To move to
the city now before the train trip south? The private car?
The house on the ocean, the . . . same mysteries, the
evasions, the perfect plotting? The removed residence,
the Rolls twice weekly into the shopping strip . . . all of
it?

LAWYER
Yes. All of it.

MISS ALICE
(Looks to JULIAN, *considers a moment)*
Are you warm now?

JULIAN
Yes ... and cold.

MISS ALICE
(Looks up to the LAWYER, *smiles faintly)*
No.

LAWYER
Then get up and come along.

MISS ALICE *(To the* LAWYER)
And all the rest of it?

LAWYER
Yes.

MISS ALICE
The years of it ... to go on? For how long?

LAWYER
Until we are replaced.

MISS ALICE
(With a tiny, tinkling laugh)
Oh God.

LAWYER
Or until everything is desert *(Shrugs)* ... on the chance
that *it* runs out before *we* do.

BUTLER
(Examining the phrenological head)
I have never even ex*a*mined phrenology.

LAWYER

But more likely till we are replaced.

JULIAN
(With a sort of quiet wonder)

I am cold at the core . . . where it burns most.

MISS ALICE *(Sad truth)*

Yes. (*Then to the* LAWYER) Yes.

LAWYER *(Almost affectionately)*

So, come now; gather yourself.

MISS ALICE (*Restrained pleading*)

But, he is still . . . ill . . .

JULIAN
(To MISS ALICE, *probably, but not* at *her)*

You wish to go away now?

MISS ALICE *(To the* LAWYER)

You see how he takes to me? You see how it *is* natural?
Poor Julian.

LAWYER

Let's go.

MISS ALICE *(To* JULIAN)

I *must* go away from you now; it is not that I wish to.
(*To* BUTLER) Butler, I have left my wig, it is upstairs . . .

BUTLER *(Rather testy)*

I'm sorry, I'm covering, I'm busy.

LAWYER *(Turning to go)*

Let me; it's such a pretty wig, becomes you so. And there
are one or two other things I'd like to check.

MISS ALICE *(Sad smile)*

The pillowcases? Put your ear against them? To eaves-
drop? Or the sheets? To see if they're still writhing?
    (The LAWYER *almost says something, thinks better
    of it, exits)*
Poor Julian.

BUTLER

Then we all are to be together.

MISS ALICE *(Small laugh)*

Oh God, you heard him: forever.

BUTLER

I like it where it's warm.

MISS ALICE

I dreaded once, when I was in my teens, that I would
grow old, look back, over the precipice, and discover that
I had not lived my life. *(Short abrupt laugh)* Oh Lord!

JULIAN
(Now a semi-coma, almost sweet)
How long wilt thou forget me, O Lord? Forever?

BUTLER

We live *some*thing.

MISS ALICE

Yes.

JULIAN

How long wilt thou hide thy face from me?

BUTLER *(To* JULIAN*)*

Psalm Thirteen.

MISS ALICE *(To* JULIAN)

Yes?

JULIAN

Yes.

BUTLER

How long shall my enemy be exalted over me?

JULIAN

Yes.

MISS ALICE

Not long.

BUTLER *(Looking at a cover)*

Consider and hear me, O Lord, my God.

JULIAN

What does it mean if the pain . . . ebbs?

BUTLER *(Considered; kindly)*

It means the agony is less.

MISS ALICE

Yes.

JULIAN *(Rueful laugh)*

Consciousness, then, is pain. *(Looks up at* MISS ALICE)
All disappointments, all treacheries. *(Ironic laugh)* Oh,
God.

BUTLER

Why are we taking separate cars, then?

MISS ALICE

Well, I might ride rubbing hips on either side with a
different lover, bouncing along, but . . . Alice, Miss

Alice would not. (*Pause*) Would I? I would not do that.
She.

BUTLER

I love you . . . not her. Or . . . quite differently.

MISS ALICE

Shhhh . . .

BUTLER

For ages, *I* look at the sheets, listen to the pillowcases,
when they're brought down, sidle into the laundry
room . . .

MISS ALICE

Don't.
           (JULIAN *makes a sound of great pain*)
Oh! . . . Oh! . . .

JULIAN
           (*Commenting on the pain*)
Dear . . . God . . . in . . . heaven . . .

MISS ALICE

Calm; be calm now.

BUTLER *(Wistful)*

But you pass through everyone, everything . . . touching
just briefly, lightly, passing.

MISS ALICE

My poor Julian. (*To the model*) Receive him? Take him
in?

JULIAN *(A little boy, scared)*

Who are you talking to?

MISS ALICE *(Breathing it)*

Alice . . .

JULIAN

Alice? Ah.

BUTLER

Will we be coming back . . . when the weather changes?

MISS ALICE *(Triste)*

Probably.

JULIAN
(Confirming the previous exchange)

Alice?

MISS ALICE

Yes.

JULIAN

Ah.

BUTLER
(Understanding what he has been told)

Ah.

(The LAWYER *enters with* MISS ALICE'S *wig)*

LAWYER

Bed stripped, mothballs lying on it like hailstones; no
sound, movement, nothing.
(Puts the wig on the phrenological head)
Do you want company, Julian? Do you want a friend?
(To MISS ALICE*)* Looks nice there. Leave it; we'll get
you another. Are you ready to go?

MISS ALICE *(Weary)*

You want me to go now?

LAWYER *(Correcting her)*

Come.

MISS ALICE

Yes. *(Begins to disengage herself)* Butler, come help me; we can't leave Julian just . . .

BUTLER

Yes. *(Moves to help her)*——

JULIAN
(As they take him by the arm)

Don't do that!

MISS ALICE

Julian, we must move you . . .

JULIAN

Don't.

LAWYER *(Without emotion)*

Leave him where he is.

JULIAN

Leave me . . . be.
(He slides along the floor, backing up against the model)
Leave me . . . where I am.

LAWYER

Good pose: leave him there.

BUTLER
(Getting a chair cushion)

Cushion.

JULIAN

All . . . hurts.

BUTLER
(Putting the cushion behind him)

Easy . . .

JULIAN

ALL HURTS!!

MISS ALICE *(Coming to him)*

Oh, my poor Julian . . .

JULIAN
(Surprisingly strong, angry)

LEAVE ME!
    (MISS ALICE *considers a moment, turns, leaves*)

LAWYER
(Walks over to JULIAN, *regards him; almost casually)*

Goodbye.

JULIAN
(Softly, but a malediction)

Instrument!

LAWYER
(Turns on his heel, walks out, saying as he goes)

Butler?

(Exits)

BUTLER
(As LAWYER *goes; abstracted)*

Yes . . . dear.

JULIAN
(Half laughed, pained incredulity)

Good . . . bye!

BUTLER *(Looks about the room)*

All in order, I think.

JULIAN *(Wistful)*

Help me?

BUTLER

My work done.

JULIAN

No?
(BUTLER *regards* JULIAN *for a moment, then walks over, bends, kisses* JULIAN *on the forehead, not a quick kiss)*

BUTLER

Goodbye, dear Julian.
(As BUTLER *exits, he closes the doors behind him)*

JULIAN
(Alone, for a moment, then, whispered)

Goodbye, dear Julian. *(Pause)* Exit . . . all. *(Softly)*
Help me . . . come back, help me. *(Pause)* HELP ME!
(Pause) No . . . no help. Kiss. A kiss goodbye, from
. . . whom? . . . Oh. From, from one . . . an . . .
arms: around me; warming. COME BACK AND HELP ME.
(Pause) If only to stay *with* me, while it . . . *if* . . .
while it happens. For . . . you, you would not have left
me if it . . . were not . . . would you? No. *(Calling to
them)* I HAVE NEVER DREAMED OF IT. NEVER . . . IM-
AGINED . . . *(To himself again)* what it would be like.
(As if they were near the door) I died once, when I was

little . . . almost, running, fell past jagged iron, noticed
. . . only when I . . . tried to get up, that my leg, left,
was torn . . . the whole thigh *and* calf . . . down.
Such . . . *searing* . . . pain? Sweet smell of blood,
screaming at the sight of it, so *far* . . . away from the
house, and in the field, all hot . . . and yellow, white
in the sun. COME BACK TO ME. Sunday, and my parents
off . . . somewhere, only my grandfather, and he . . .
OFF: SOMEWHERE: mousing with the dog. All the way
down . . . bone, flesh, meat, moving. Help me, Grandfather! "Ere I die, ere life ebbs." *(Laughs softly)* Oh,
Christ. *(Little boy)* Grandfather? Mousing? Come to me:
Julian bleeds, leg torn, from short pants to shoe, bone,
meat open to the sun; come to him. *(Looks at the model,
above and behind him)* Ahhhh. Will no one come? *(Looks
at the ceiling)* High; high walls . . . summit. *(Eyes on
his leg)* Belly . . . not leg. Come, grandfather! Not leg,
belly! Doublebutton. Pinpoint, searing . . . pain? "If
you . . . if you die." Are you sleeping, not mousing?
Sleeping on the sunporch? Hammocking? Yes. "If I die
before *you* wake, will the Lord deign *your* soul take?"
Grandfather? *(Cry of pain, then)* Oh . . . GOD! "I come
to thee, in agony." *(Cry to the void)* HELP . . . ME!
(Pause) No help. Stitch it up like a wineskin! Hold the
wine in. Stitch it up. *(Sweet reminiscence)* And every day,
put him in the sun, quarter over, for the whole stitched
leg . . . to bake, in the healing sun. Green? Yes, a little,
but that's the medicine. And keep him out of the fields,
chuckle, chuckle. And every day, swinging in the sun,
baking; good. Aching all the while, but good. The cat
comes, sniffs it, won't stay. Finally . . . stays; lies in
the bend, doubling it, purring, breathing, soaking in the
sun, as the leg throbs, aches, heals. "How will I know
thee, O Lord, when I am in thy sight? How will I know
thee?" By my *faith*. Ah, I see. *(Furious, shouting at the
roof)* BY FAITH? THE FAITH I HAVE SHOWN THEE? BENT

MYSELF? What may we avoid! Not birth! Growing up?
Yes. Maturing? Oh, *God!* Growing old, and? . . . yes,
growing old; but not the last; merely when. *(Sweet singsong)* But to live again, be born once more, sure in the
sight of . . . *(Shouts again)* THERE IS NO ONE! *(Turns
his head toward the closed doors, sadly)* Unless you are
listening there. Unless you have left me, tiptoed off some,
stood whispering, smothered giggles, and . . . silently
returned, your ears pressed against, or . . . or one eye
into the crack so that the air smarts it sifting through.
HAVE YOU COME BACK? HAVE YOU NOT LEFT ME? *(Pause)*
No. No one. Out in the night . . . nothing. Night? No;
what then? IS IT NIGHT . . . OR DAY? *(Great weariness)*
Or does it matter? No. How long wilt thou forget me, O
Lord? Forever? How long wilt thou hide thy face from
me? How long shall my enemy . . . I . . . can . . .
barely . . . feel. Which is a sign. A change, at any rate.
(To the rooftops again) I DO NOT UNDERSTAND, O LORD,
MY GOD, WHAT THOU WILT HAVE OF ME! *(More conver-
sational)* I have never dreamed of it, never imagined
what it would be like. I have—oh, yes—dwelt *(Laughs at
the word)* . . . dwelt . . . on the *fact* of it, the . . .
principle, but I have not imagined dying. Death . . .
yes. Not being, but not the act of . . . dying? ALICE!?
(Laughs softly) Oh, Alice, why hast *thou* forsaken me?
(Leans his head back to see the model) Hast thou? Alice?
Hast thou forsaken me . . . with . . . all the others?
(Laughs again) Come bring me my slippers and my pipe,
and push the dog into the room. Bring me my slippers,
the sacramental wine, *(Little boy)* my cookie? *(Usual
again)* . . . come bring me my ease, come sit with me
. . . and watch me as I die. Alice? ALICE!? *(To himself)*
There is nothing; there is no one. *(Wheedling a little)*
Come talk to me; come sit by my right hand . . . *on*
the one hand . . . come sit with me and hold my . . .
what? Then come and talk; tell me how it goes, Alice.

(Laughs) "Raise high the roofbeam, for the bridegroom comes." Oh, what a priesthood is this! Oh, what a range of duties, and such parishioners, and such a chapel for my praise. *(Turns some, leans toward the model, where the chapel light shines)* Oh, what a priesthood, see my chapel, how it . . .

> *(Suddenly the light in the chapel in the model goes out.* JULIAN *starts, makes a sound of surprise and fear)*

Alice? . . . God? SOMEONE? Come to Julian as he . . . ebbs.

> *(We begin to hear it now, faintly at first, slowly growing, so faintly at first it is subliminal: the heartbeat . . . thump* thump *. . . thump* thump *. . . And the breathing . . . the intake taking one thump-thump, the exhaling the next.* JU-LIAN *neither senses nor hears it yet, however)*

Come, comfort him, warm him. He has not been a willful man . . . Oh, willful in his . . . cry to serve, but gentle, would not cause pain, but bear it, *would* bear it . . . has, even. Not much, I suppose. One man's share is not . . . another's burden. *(Notices the wig on the phrenological head; crawls a bit toward it; half kneels in front of it)* Thou art my bride? Thou? For thee have I done my life? Grown to love, entered in, bent . . . accepted? For thee? Is that the . . . awful humor? Art thou the true arms, when the warm flesh I touched . . . rested against, was . . . nothing? And *she* . . . was not real? Is thy stare the true look? Unblinking, outward, through, to some horizon? And her eyes . . . warm, accepting, were they . . . not real? Art thou my bride? *(To the ceiling again)* Ah God! Is that the humor? THE ABSTRACT? . . . REAL? THE REST? . . . FALSE? *(To himself, with terrible irony)* It is what I have wanted, have insisted on. Have nagged . . . for *(Looking about the room, raging)* IS THIS MY PRIESTHOOD, THEN? THIS WORLD? THEN COME AND SHOW THYSELF! BRIDE? GOD?

(Silence; we hear the heartbeats and the breathing some)

SHOW THYSELF! I DEMAND THEE! *(JULIAN crawls back toward the model; faces it, back to the audience, addresses it)* SHOW THYSELF! FOR THEE I HAVE GAMBLED . . . MY SOUL? I DEMAND THY PRESENCE. ALICE!

> *(The sounds become louder now, as, in the model, the light fades in the bedroom, begins to move across an upper story. JULIAN's reaction is a muffled cry)*

AGHHH! *(On his hands and knees he backs off a little from the model, still staring at it)* You . . . thou . . . art . . . coming to me? *(Frightened and angry)* ABSTRACTION? . . . ABSTRACTION! . . . *(Sad, defeated)* Art coming to me. *(A shivered prayer, quick)* How long wilt thou forget me, O Lord? Forever? How long wilt thou hide thy face from me? . . . Consider and hear me, O Lord, my God. *(Shouted now)* CONSIDER AND HEAR ME, O LORD, MY GOD. LIGHTEN MY EYES LEST I SLEEP THE SLEEP OF DEATH.

> *(The lights keep moving; the sounds become louder)*

BUT I HAVE TRUSTED IN THY MERCY, O LORD. HOW LONG WILT THOU FORGET ME? *(Softly, whining)* How long wilt thou hide thy face from me? COME, BRIDE! COME, GOD! COME!

> *(The breathing and heartbeats are much, much louder now. The lights descend a stairway in the model. JULIAN turns, backs against the model, his arms way to the side of him)*

Alice? *(Fear and trembling)* Alice? ALICE? MY GOD, WHY HAST THOU FORSAKEN ME?

> *(A great shadow, or darkening, fills the stage; it is the shadow of a great presence filling the room. The area on JULIAN and around him stays in some light, but, for the rest, it is as if ink were moving through paper toward a focal*

point. The sounds become enormous. JULIAN
*is aware of the presence in the room, "sees" it,
in the sense that his eyes, his head move to all
areas of the room, noticing his engulfment. He
almost-whispers loudly)*

The bridegroom waits for thee, my Alice . . . is thine. O
Lord, my God, I have awaited thee, have served thee in
thy . . . ALICE? *(His arms are wide, should resemble a
crucifixion. With his hands on the model, he will raise his
body some, backed full up against it)* ALICE? . . . GOD?

(The sounds are deafening. JULIAN *smiles faintly)*

I accept thee, Alice, for thou art come to me. God, Alice
. . . I accept thy will.

(Sounds continue. JULIAN *dies, head bows,
body relaxes some, arms stay wide in the crucifixion. Sounds continue thusly: thrice after the
death . . .* thump thump *thump* thump *thump*
thump. *Absolute silence for two beats. The
lights on* JULIAN *fade slowly to black. Only
then, when all is black, does the curtain slowly
fall)*